AFTER

THIS MANNER,

PRAY

AFTER

THIS MANNER,

PRAY

Understanding the Power of

The Lord's Prayer

By J. Mark Copeland

Bridge Publishing, Inc.

All Scripture references in this book are taken from the New International Version of the Bible unless otherwise noted.

Some key exegetical and foundational material is cited as noted from *The Gospel of Matthew,* (Volume I : The Daily Bible Study Series) (Revised Edition), by William Barclay.

After This Manner, Pray
ISBN 0-88270-653-5
Library of Congress No. 92-070135

Published by:
Bridge Publishing, Inc.
2500 Hamilton Blvd.
South Plainfield, NJ 07080

Printed in the United States of America.

This book is dedicated in loving memory
to my earthly father,
JAMES EDWARD COPELAND,
who like my Heavenly Father
was a faithful provider

and

in loving memory
to my earthly mother,
ANNIE EUNICE COPELAND,
whose prayers and love and support
encouraged me and sustained me.

Table of Contents

Foreword

I am convinced that the Christian church has recently entered the most thrilling decade of its history. The current spread of the Kingdom of God and the concomitant harvest of souls is exceeding anything previously imagined. Justice and righteousness are being preached as never before. In fact, I see signs that the great revival which we have longed for and long awaited may not be far away.

The basic foundation to this amazing era is prayer. Prayer is the believer's weapon of spiritual warfare par excellence. True, many pastors and Christian laypeople are not yet aware of the worldwide prayer movement, but most soon will be. Mark Copeland is well aware of it. He is one of today's cutting edge Christian leaders whom God is using to see that others become aware, and *After This Manner, Pray* will be one of our chief resources for years to come.

I am delighted that Mark decided to make his deep insights on the Lord's Prayer accessible to all of us through this book. Nothing could be more helpful for God's people everywhere than understanding why the Lord's Prayer is the Master's prayer outline, and then learning how to incorporate it into their daily prayer lives.

Some years ago my own personal prayer life was revolutionized when I began using the Lord's Prayer as my prayer outline. Since then it puzzles me why every Christian doesn't do it since we desire to be followers of Jesus, and Jesus gave the Lord's Prayer to His disciples in response to their request, "Lord, teach us to pray." Just to make sure that they understood it then and that we would understand it centuries later, Jesus gave the same prayer outline twice, one recorded in Matthew and one in Luke. There were some 18 months time lapse between the two occasions.

I have read other books on the Lord's Prayer, and they have been very helpful. However, none had the depth and theological insights which Mark Copeland's book has. In this book you will find a provocative combination of rationale, motivation, biblical insight, and practical application to everyday life that you will not find elsewhere. Reading this book is an enjoyable experience for spiritually-minded believers, and an avenue toward a deeper and more intimate relationship with the Father.

There is a difference between *saying* the Lord's Prayer and *praying* the Lord's Prayer. With great anointing, Mark Copeland teaches us how to pray it and how to see God's power increased in our daily lives.

C. Peter Wagner
Fuller Theological Seminary
Pasadena, California

Preface

The Spirit of God is speaking a timely word to the church about the importance of prayer. He is speaking about the high priority that believers must give to prayer if they are to lead victorious Christian lives and effectively fulfill the Great Commission. This is evident from the fact that many of God's choice servants who have ears to hear what the Spirit is saying to the church have in recent years used the printed page to call Christians back to praying as Jesus taught us to pray. Their writings have offered helpful contributions toward understanding, appreciating and utilizing Jesus' inspired outline of prayer which we have come to call the Lord's Prayer.

Over the past twelve years, at least five of God's choice servants have authored book-length treatments of the Lord's Prayer encouraging Christians to find in its petitions new vitality for their prayers and for their witness. First, Everett L. Fullam encouraged us to let the Lord's Prayer become the basis for living all that we as Christians believe.(1) Second, Larry Lea challenged us to take time away from the busy-ness of our daily routine to tarry with the Lord daily for at least an hour of meaningful, life-changing communion.(2) Third, Paul Yonggi Cho invited us to find answers to our questions about what to pray for and how to pray by making Jesus our mentor and instructor in the discipline of prayer.(3) Fourth, Douglas F. Kelly inspired us to petition God in prayer with the sincerity and confidence of a child making request of his father.(4) Finally, Rita Bennett excited us with the prospect of finding an inner wholeness that is contagious as we prayerfully embrace God's grace which assures us of his love, his protection and his provision.(5)

With so many helpful book-length treatments of the Lord's Prayer available, the reader may well wonder why another is being offered. In answer, let me say that the Spirit of God will continue to impress upon the church the need to make the Lord's Prayer the basis for our prayer lives until its central petition has been granted; that is, until God's kingdom comes to the earth with the effect that His will is done in the human community as perfectly as it is done in heaven. Thus the Lord's Prayer is a prayer for the salvation of the lost, the sanctification of the redeemed, and the full consummation of God's kingdom reign on earth to be ushered in at the return of Christ.

I have written this book about the Lord's Prayer because it is a prayer that we must persist in praying until it is answered. We must continue to petition for the coming of God's kingdom and the establishment of His will until it becomes evident in our daily living that God's laws are written upon our hearts and that we obey Him always with an inner compulsion of love. We must persist in praying this prayer until God unleashes an end-time, world-wide revival that will sweep multitudes into the kingdom causing the glory of God to cover the earth as the waters cover the sea. We must persist in praying this prayer until our prayers usher in the return of Jesus Christ and the complete establishment of the unchallenged reign of God over His people.

This book emphasizes the centrality of the kingdom of God in all of our praying and the importance of our prayers for the ushering in of God's kingdom. As we make God's kingdom the center of our prayers, our prayers will be the vehicle by which God brings His kingdom reign into our lives and our world.

I trust that your reading of this book will impart to you a love for God's kingdom and a longing for its ultimate manifestation among humankind at Christ's return. Such love and such longing will impel you to a life of prayer and sevice that will exemplify, propagate and celebrate the reign of God among His people even as you eagerly anticipate the establishment of His ultimate reign over all.

Notes

1. Fullam, Everett, and Bob Slosser. *Living the Lord's Prayer.* Tarrytown, New York: Fleming H. Revell Company, 1980.

2. Used by permission of Creation House, Lake Mary, Florida, *Could You Not Tarry One Hour?* by Larry Lea. Copyright ©1987.

3. Cho, Paul Yonggi. *Praying With Jesus.* Altamonte Springs, Florida: Creation House, 1987.

4. Kelly, Douglas F., and Caroline S. Kelly. *If God Already Knows, Why Pray?* Brentwood, Tennessee: Woglumuth & Hyatt, Publishers, Inc., 1989.

5. Bennett, Rita. *Inner Wholeness Through The Lord's Prayer.* Tarrytown, New York: Fleming H. Revell Company, 1991.

Introduction

"Much prayer, much power; little prayer, little power; no prayer, no power." With these words an inveterate missionary advised a young evangelist seeking counsel for the success of his ministry. With these words all Christians should be advised as we seek counsel for success in fulfilling our Lord's Great Commission. Regardless of what part our individual ministries might play in the overall task of reaching the world with the gospel, a primary prerequisite to an effective ministry is an effective prayer life.

Not understanding the biblical principles that govern prayer has caused many Christians to be ineffective in prayer. The consequence is that such individuals regress from ineffective prayer into the sin of prayerlessness. Such prayerlessness stifles their ability to receive the continuous flow of divine power necessary to be effective in God's service. It makes them fruitless Christians. If their plight is to be reversed so that their lives become fruitful and effective in God's service, they must understand just why their prayer lives have been fruitless and just what measures must be taken to cultivate an effective prayer life. This book is offered as a contribution toward such an understanding.

At the outset, let me suggest that perhaps the greatest hindrance to an effective prayer life is a lack of certainty concerning God's will in the matters about which prayer is offered. If we do not know God's will about the concerns that we bring before Him in prayer, we will not be able to pray with precision and conviction. Our petitions will not be offered to God with the confidence which is of the essence of faith. Consequently, our prayers will be unheard and unanswered.

Many deal with the problem of uncertainty concerning God's will in the matters about which they pray by appending onto their requests the words "if it be Thy will." Submission to the will of God should always be the heartbeat of prayer. Jesus exemplified such submission for us when He prayed repeatedly in the Garden of Gethsemane, "Yet not as I will, but as you will" (Matthew 26:39). But God does not want His people to be ignorant of His will. Paul exhorted the Christians of Ephesus, with these words: "Therefore do not be foolish, but understand what the Lord's will is" (Ephesians 5:17). While this passage primarily concerns God's will about how we should live, it is evident from Scripture that we should also know God's will regarding the concerns for which we pray. Such enlightened prayer gives us confidence that God truly hears our petitions and grants our requests. Consider these words penned by the Apostle John: "This is the confidence we have in approaching God: that if we ask anything according to his will, he hears us. And if we know that he hears us—whatever we ask—we know that we have what we asked of him" (1 John 5:14,15).

The Apostle John exhorts us to approach God in prayer with a confidence that results from knowing that the petitions of our prayers are in perfect accord with God's will. But how can we know with certainty that we are praying according to God's will? We can be assured that our prayers are aligned with God's will whenever we pray in agreement with His Word. God's Word and His will are one. God will not say one thing and will another.

If praying in agreement with God's Word is praying in accordance with His will, then the best means to developing an effective prayer life is to learn scriptural praying. Scriptural praying is allowing the revelation of God's will as revealed through His Word to become the foundation and basis of our prayer lives.

If our prayer lives are to be revitalized so that prayer becomes both fruitful and fulfilling, we must make it a discipline to look regularly to God's Word for instruction and guidance in prayer. We must discipline ourselves to make the revelation of God's will as revealed through His Word both the foundation and the basis of all of our prayers. There is no better way to do this than to carefully study and apply the principles and insights concerning prayer that are communicated to us through the Lord's Prayer. Jesus gave this prayer to His disciples in response to their request, "Lord, teach us to pray . . ." (Luke 11:1). By virtue of its inclusion in Scripture, it is an inspired prayer. More than *an* inspired prayer, it is *the* inspired prayer which Jesus has given to guide His followers in praying in accord with God's perfect will.

As modern day disciples of Jesus, we would greatly benefit from making the Lord's Prayer the basis for our daily prayer lives. This fact is more than adequately demonstrated through the testimony of Paul Yonggi Cho, a Korean pastor who has learned the value of prayer in general and of the Lord's Prayer in particular. With God's blessing upon his ministry—his church has grown to be the world's largest church.

Pastor Cho began his ministry more than twenty-five years ago in a poor Korean neighborhood. His work has now grown into the present day Yoido Full Gospel Church of Seoul, Korea—a church whose active membership now exceeds 600,000 people. What is the secret behind the success of his ministry? His answer is simply stated, "I pray and I obey."

I have attended two meetings at which Cho was a guest speaker—one in Pasadena, California, and one in Virginia Beach, Virginia. In both settings, Cho's primary goal was to encourage Christians to take prayer more seriously than ever. To spur believers to pray, Cho credits his personal success in ministry to regularly spending between three and five hours in daily prayer. And what is the basis for Cho's prayer life? It is the Lord's Prayer, which he calls his "prayer track." Cho refers to the six petitions of the Lord's Prayer as the "laps" that he faithfully runs in daily prayer.

As with Cho, so with us. Making the Lord's Prayer the basis for our prayer lives will assure that God blesses our lives and ministries with success. It is in praying in accordance with the insights and directives that emerge from the Lord's Prayer that we can know for certain that we are praying according to God's will. This will enable us to present our petitions to God with confidence. We will know that our prayers are heard and answered. The time we spend in prayer will not be time spent in vain. It will effectively bring God's kingdom and His will to bear in our lives and in the lives of those for whom we pray.

How do we make the Lord's Prayer the basis of our prayer lives? I believe that we should do so in two ways. First, we should reflectively pray the prayer verbatim from time to time. Through such reflective praying, we permit the Holy Spirit to enlarge our spiritual understanding of the meaning behind each petition of the prayer. In this way we allow God to speak to us through the Lord's Prayer even as we are praying the words of the prayer to Him. Second, we should treat each petition of the Lord's Prayer as a topic for amplification and elaboration in prayer. For The Lord's Prayer is not intended to be prayed verbatim only. It is actually given to us as our Lord's inspired outline of prayer.

I first learned that Jesus intended the Lord's Prayer to be an outline of prayer from the writings of Larry Lea, founding pastor of Church on the Rock of Rockwall, Texas.(1) Lea points out that the Jewish rabbis during the first century presented their teaching in outline form. It was the responsibility of their disciples to take the outline, do their homework and enlarge upon what they had learned. Jesus was a teacher of Israel whom the disciples called Rabbi. It would stand to reason, then, that He would respond to their desire to be taught how to pray by giving them an outline of prayer. This is what He gave them in the Lord's Prayer.

To bolster the view that the Lord's Prayer is intended to be an outline of prayer, Lea cites the research of Brad Young. Young's, *The Jewish Background of the Lord's Prayer,* points out that written prayers of early Christians that are based upon the Lord's Prayer and require approximately one hour to pray still exist.(2) What is the significance of Young's point? It confirms our position that early Christians considered the Lord's Prayer to be not a model prayer but an outline of prayer.

As an outline of prayer, the Lord's Prayer is truly comprehensive. As Bible commentator William Barclay points out, this prayer brings the whole of God to the whole of life. (See Matthew 6:9-13.)(3) It is God the Father whose name we hallow and for whose kingdom we pray (vs. 9-10). He provides us with our daily bread (vs. 11). Thus *God the Father* meets the pressing needs of the *present.* Through God the Son we receive the forgiveness of past sins that would hinder our walk with the Lord (vs. 12). Thus *God the Son* effectively deals with our needs relating to the *past.* Through God the Holy Spirit we are delivered from overbearing temptations and from the devices of the evil one who would threaten to undo us (vs. 13). Thus *God the Holy Spirit* assures our security and well-being for the *future.* We see the wisdom of Jesus in giving us this inspired outline of prayer. In praying the Lord's Prayer, we address all of God and lay before Him all of life.

In this book, we will carefully study the Lord's Prayer as our Lord's inspired outline of prayer. We will endeavor to understand its every petition in the context of Scripture and of life. The insights that we gain from our study will, if we let them, transform our prayer lives to the end that our prayers are prayed with confidence and effectiveness.

We will present our study in three parts. We will concern ourselves with the *context,* the *center* and the *circumference* of the Lord's Prayer. Allow me to say a word about each part of this structure.

In part one, we will endeavor to learn about prayer from the *context* of the Lord's Prayer as it is given to us in the gospels of Matthew and Luke. For the purposes of this study, we will set our parameters to include Matthew 5-6 and Luke 10-11. Through this analysis, we will see how Jesus dealt with the problem of ineffective prayer by attacking the spiritual forces and religious traditions that threatened to undo prayer and by teaching His disciples both why they should pray and how they should pray. This section will help us to align our perception of prayer with God's and will impart to us practical wisdom on wholesome and unwholesome prayer habits.

Parts two and three will focus upon the text of the Lord's Prayer as it is given in Matthew's gospel (6:9-13). In part two, we will direct our attention to the *center* of the Lord's Prayer (vss. 9-10). Here we will concern ourselves with the opening address and the first three petitions of the prayer that concern God and His kingdom. We will see that top priority in prayer is to be given to worshiping God and petitioning for the coming of His kingdom to the earth. As we learn to make God and His kingdom the central focus of our praying, we will learn the secret of effective prayer.

In part three, we will expand our focus to the *circumference* of prayer (vss. 11-13). Here we will direct our attention to the final three petitions of the prayer and the closing doxology that concern themselves with the meeting of our needs and with ascribing glory to God. To put God and His kingdom at the center of our praying is to relegate our needs to the circumference of prayer. Petitions for the meeting of our needs take secondary priority, but, they are not excluded from the prayer as unimportant. Petitioning for the meeting of our needs provides God opportunity to demonstrate His love and goodness to us and so advance His glory.

With this schematic before us, we are ready to embark upon a study of our Lord's inspired outline of prayer. Let us commit ourselves at the outset to so familiarize ourselves with the Lord's "prayer track" that we can run it daily with understanding and spiritual sensitivity. As we do, we will be all the better equipped to run the race that is set before us to the glory of God and for the furtherance of His kingdom.

Notes

1. Used by permission of Creation House, Lake Mary, Florida, from *Could You Not Tarry One Hour?* by Larry Lea. Copyright © 1987, pp. 50,51.copyright 1987, pp. 50,51.

2. Ibid., p. 51.

3. From *The Gospel of Matthew*, (Volume I: The Daily Study Bible Series) (Revised Edition), by William Barclay. Copyright © 1975 William Barclay. Used by permission of Westminster/John Knox Press and Saint Andrew Press, pp. 199,200.

PART ONE

The Context Of

The Lord's Prayer

Matthew 5, 6

Luke 10, 11

Chapter One

The Recovery Of Prayer

In the early 1920s, a group of individuals who were socially well-to-do, intellectually acute and racially prejudiced arose in our country. They believed that the white race was superior to the black and intended to use their influence with the government to curtail the influx of black people into the country and to limit the birth rate of those already here. They solved the "problem" of the influx of black people into the country by working toward the passing of restrictive immigration laws. They also worked to limit the birthrate among the blacks already here through the promotion of sterilization legislation. They knew that if they could force sterilization upon black women who had already had a couple of children, they would be able to control population growth in black communities.(1)

Throughout the centuries, a similar sinister force has been at work wherever the gospel has been preached. The powers of darkness are prejudiced against Christians and do not want any more children born into God's family. In an effort to curtail new births, they have devised a scheme. They will work for sterility in the Christian family. And how will they do this? Simple! They will work toward the seduction of prayer.

Prayer is the key to the spiritual fertility of the Church. Just as human love expresses itself in sexual intimacy that results in the growth of the human family, love for God expresses itself in intimate communion with God that results in the growth of the Christian family. Prayer is communion with God through which God's kingdom comes to earth.

Jesus was concerned about the forces at work in the world seeking to seduce prayer and sterilize its effects. He aimed at saving prayer from these forces and restoring it to its intended potency. For this reason, He addressed the danger signs evident in the prayer lives of the religious establishment of His day with a warning to His disciples not to be seduced by such ineffectual prayer habits. Then He gave them His inspired outline of prayer. Following this model would revitalize their communion with God and make their lives fruitful in the enlarging of God's kingdom upon the earth.

This chapter focuses upon Jesus' program for the recovery of prayer from the subtle forces aimed at its seduction and sterilization. Our attention will be directed primarily to the immediate context of the Lord's Prayer as it is given in Matthew's gospel. Our discussion will be presented under two headings: the seduction of prayer and the salvation of prayer.

The Seduction Of Prayer

What do we mean by the seduction of prayer? To seduce means "to allure" and so "to lead astray." It means "to draw aside from the path of rectitude and duty."(2) The seduction of prayer takes place anytime one is allured or led astray from a right understanding of prayer and from a proper practice of prayer.

The seduction of prayer is not a process by which one loses interest in prayer and so falls to a state of prayerlessness. It is a process by which one is led to embrace a wrong understanding of prayer, which inevitably leads to an improper practice of prayer. How can we recognize this seduction of prayer? It is evident when our prayer lives have an appearance of communion with God but lack the substance of such communion. Rather than bringing us closer to God, this wrong understanding of prayer drives us further away from God.

As the context of the Lord's Prayer in Matthew's gospel reveals, Jesus was concerned about the seduction of prayer among both Jews and Gentiles. He warned His disciples to avoid the tendencies in both camps to wrongly understand and improperly practice prayer. From His warnings, we can decipher three characteristics of prayer that has become prey to seductive forces. The seduction of prayer results in:

1. prayer without the heart
2. prayer without the will
3. prayer without the mind

First of all, the seduction of prayer results in prayer without the heart. Prayer should always involve a bowing of the heart before God. It should always entail humbling oneself before God, casting oneself upon His mercy and receiving His grace for the meeting of one's needs and the granting of one's petitions. Prayer without such genuine humility is prayer without the heart.

Jesus warned against prayer without the heart. He said, "And when you pray, do not be like the hypocrites, for they love to pray standing in the synagogues and on the street corners to be seen by men. I tell you the truth, they have received their reward in full" (Matthew 6:5). Such people as Jesus described here were not bowing their hearts before God in humility. Rather, they were exalting themselves before men in pride.

The hypocrisy of prayer without humility was easy to spot among the Jews of Jesus' day. Orthodox Judaism specified three times per day that were to be devoted to prayer. Every believing Jew was to pray at 9:00 a.m., 12:00 p.m. and 3:00 p.m. Any Jewish person who wanted to flaunt his spirituality might schedule himself to be in a public place surrounded by many people at the hour of prayer. He would then stand still, raise his arms into the air, turn the palms of his hands heavenward, bow his head and begin to pray with a display of great devotion.(4) Although onlookers might view this public prayer as a sign of deep devotion, Jesus called it hypocrisy. Why? Because it was prayer without humility. To God, it was prayer without the heart.

We must be on guard against prayer without the heart. It is easy to become self-conscious about prayer. I've heard people say that they do not want to be called on to pray in a public place without being notified in advance so that they can prepare for it. I've heard others willingly pray in public but later apologize about the quality of their prayer. These are just two examples of the tendency to use prayer as a means of impressing others with one's spirituality rather than as an opportunity to humbly approach God's throne. Such prayer without humility is prayer without the heart.

Second, the seduction of prayer results in prayer without the will. If prayer without the heart is prayer lacking humility, then prayer without the will is prayer lacking sincerity. Anytime we pray prayers that we don't really mean, we've engaged in prayer without the will.

The Orthodox Jews of Jesus' day could easily fall into the trap of praying without the will. Not only did scribal tradition require that they pray at three set times daily, but they were also required to pray much from memory. One such prayer was the *Shema*, which pledged whole-hearted love and devotion to God, promised continuous meditation upon His law and rehearsed the blessings for obedience and the curses for disobedience to His commands. This prayer was to be said twice daily—once in the morning before 9:00 a.m. and once in the evening before 9:00 p.m.(5) Orthodox Jews also prayed the *Shemoneh 'esreh*, or The Eighteen, a liturgy that originally consisted of eighteen short prayers appealing to God for mercy and favor. This liturgy of prayers was to be prayed three times per day—once in the morning, once in the afternoon and once in the evening.(6)

You can just imagine that having to pray eighteen or more memorized prayers every day could easily become a hindrance to the vitality and sincerity of one's prayer life. One could become preoccupied with praying words that do not express his true sentiments. He understands what he is praying but doesn't truly mean what he is praying. He is praying without the will.

Praying without the will is a subtle form of the seduction of prayer. Those who have disciplined themselves to set aside specific times for daily prayer, and specific guidelines to follow in their prayers must especially guard against this snare. On those days when they are energetic and ready to pray, they will certainly find that their prayers are offered sincerely. At other times when prayer requires more personal discipline, however, they may find that following the normal routine puts them in the position of praying words that do not express the true sentiments of their will. At such times, it would be wise to be less rigid and more spontaneous in prayer. We must mean what we pray if our prayers are to be fruitful. We must avoid the trap of praying without the will.

Third, the seduction of prayer results in prayer without the mind. The ultimate evidence of the seduction of prayer is apparent when prayer becomes thoughtless and mechanical. If we don't engage our minds in our praying, then we certainly won't engage our wills or our hearts in prayer.

Jesus was concerned about mindless praying. He said, "And when you pray, do not keep on babbling like pagans, for they think they will be heard because of their many words. Do not be like them, for your Father knows what you need before you ask him" (Matthew 6:7,8). Other translations of these verses indicate that Jesus warned against the use of "vain repetitions" (KJV), "empty phrases" (RSV) or "meaningless words" (TEV). It is not so much long prayers or repetitious prayers that Jesus warned against. Jesus Himself spent long periods of time in prayer (see Mark 1:35) and once prayed the same prayer three times in succession. (See Matthew 26:36-44.) Rather, Jesus is concerned about the danger of thinking that prayer is efficacious because of its repetition and does not, therefore, need to engage the mind at all.

Jesus attributed mindless praying to pagans or Gentiles. (See Matthew 6:6.) In Jesus' day, the non-Jewish world often treated prayer as a form of magical incantation in which the sheer number of repetitions of certain words or phrases produced the desired effect.(7) Since the words themselves were believed to contain such power, it was not deemed important to think about the prayer. It was only necessary to say the prayer. This was mindless praying in its ultimate form.

How might we fall into the trap of mindless praying? We can fall into this trap by *saying* our prayers rather than *praying* our prayers. Dr. Robert Cook says, "All of us have one routine prayer in our system; and once we get rid of it, then we can really start to pray!"(8) Routine prayer can easily become mindless praying. One humorous example makes the point. On one memorable occasion, my mother said the blessing at dinner time. A minute or so later, she asked, "Who would like to say the blessing?" It took my dad, my brother and me to convince her that she had already said the blessing. Because grace is a routine prayer, it is easy to say it thoughtlessly. We must be careful not to pray without the mind.

The seduction of prayer may manifest itself in prayer without the heart, prayer without the will, or even prayer without the mind. Jesus warned us to guard against each of these pitfalls of prayer. Having told us how *not* to pray, Jesus then instructed us how *to* pray. This brings us to consider the salvation of prayer.

The Salvation Of Prayer

One definition of the word save is "to rescue . . . . from danger."(9) The salvation of prayer is the process by which prayer is rescued from the danger of seduction. We have already deciphered from Jesus' teaching in the context of the Lord's Prayer three manifestations of the seduction of prayer. This same body of teaching contains three lessons that will assure the salvation of prayer. If we are to properly practice prayer, we must understand three points:

1. the object of prayer
2. the focus of prayer
3. the effect of prayer

First of all, if our prayers are to be salvaged from seduction, we must understand the object of prayer. The object of prayer refers to the one to whom prayer is addressed. To whom do we pray? Jesus said, "But when you pray, go into your room, close the door and pray to your Father who is unseen" (Matthew 6:6). God alone is the object of our prayers.

Everybody knows that prayer is talking to
people often have difficulty applying this simpl
in their prayer lives. Rather than prayer being co
ion with God, prayer is often offered without a proper sense of the presence of God. The result is that prayer becomes either a form of public address or of private monologue.

Prayer as public address is portrayed as the prayer offered by hypocrites who "love to pray standing in the synagogues" (Matthew 6:5). During the local synagogue services, one person would be asked to stand before the congregation and to lead in prayer. To be asked to lead in this public prayer was considered to be a mark of distinction.(10) The one asked to pray might be moved by the respect given him and by the formality of the occasion to present his prayer as though it were just as much a public address as the teaching of the rabbi to follow. To this situation, Jesus offered a corrective: pray to God only—not to the people.

Prayer offered without a proper focus upon the presence of God as the object of one's prayer can also take the form of private monologue. We're all familiar with the parable of the Pharisee and the publican. The Pharisee prayed self-righteously, bragging on his piety and devotion. The publican prayed in humility and repentance, appealing to God's mercy. The Bible tells us something interesting about the Pharisee's prayer. We read that he prayed "about himself" (Luke 18:11). The NIV footnote indicates that this could be made to read that he prayed "to" himself. The Jerusalem Bible actually renders the passage as saying that he "prayed this prayer to himself." This

Pharisee was not conscious of the presence of a gracious God hearing and receiving his prayer. He was conscious only of himself and his self-righteousness. Therefore, he did not really pray to God. He prayed to himself. His prayer was private monologue. To this tendency Jesus would say, "Pray to God alone and not to yourself."

When we get up from the place of prayer, do we know that God has heard us? Do we know that He has received our prayer? Do we expect to receive His answer to our prayer? If we cannot say "yes" to these questions, then we have prayed without an awareness of the presence of God. Therefore, we have not truly prayed to God. We must learn to wait upon God in prayer until we know His presence. Then we must pray in childlike faith to the God who is present. Only so can we pray with the right object of prayer.

Second, if our prayers are to be salvaged from seduction, we need to be clear on the focus of prayer. And what should be the focus of our prayer? It should be the kingdom of God. Both the context of the Lord's Prayer in Matthew's gospel and the Lord's Prayer itself are concerned preeminently with the kingdom of God.

The context of the Lord's Prayer is the Sermon on the Mount. (See Matthew 5-7.) Many Bible expositors refer to the Sermon on the Mount as "The Law of the Kingdom." Its contents are really a description of those who are true citizens of God's kingdom. We read of the blessedness of their lives, the appeal of their witness, the sincerity of their ethics and the humility and constancy of their devotion. All of these qualities are produced in the lives of people by God's kingdom rule in their hearts.

The text of the Lord's Prayer itself is also concerned preeminently with the kingdom of God. God's kingdom is the focus of the prayer. The prayer first addresses the King of heaven and gives honor to His name. Then we ask for God's kingdom to come to earth so that His will may be done perfectly in the human community. Then, in successive petitions, we appeal to the King for provision, for pardon and for protection. Finally, we honor the King again by a doxology that expresses faith in His kingdom, His power and His glory. Throughout the prayer, the focus remains upon the kingdom of God.

We must make the kingdom of God the focus of our praying. We do that when our prayers aim at bringing God's will to be done upon the earth as it is in heaven. Robert Law says, "Prayer is a mighty instrument, not for getting man's will done in heaven, but for getting God's will done in earth."(11)

Now this is an important point to grasp in understanding the value of prayer. People often talk as though God's perfect will is going to be done regardless of whether we pray or not. But this simply is not so. When the kingdom of God is the focus of our praying, the will of God established in the earth is the fruit of our praying.

When God's kingdom is the focus of prayer, God's will is the fruit of prayer. One of the most fascinating testimonies of this fact that I have read in recent months comes from John Dawson, the Southwest United States director of Youth With A Mission.(12)

In an interview with Steven Lawson of *Charisma and Christian Life* magazine, John Dawson relates a memorable experience through which a delegation of young missionaries learned the power of prayer to bring God's kingdom to bear in the life of a city. In 1978, Dawson took a group of two hundred young missionaries to Cordoba, Argentina. Their assignment was to mingle with the crowds who had come to attend the world soccer finals, to share the gospel with them through personal witnessing and the distribution of tracts and to lead as many as possible to Christ.

The initial efforts of Dawson and his fellow-workers to evangelize in Cordoba were futile. Nobody seemed willing to hear their good news. Those who took their gospel tracts tossed them aside without reading them. Discouraged and frustrated, the young missionaries decided to retreat to a monastery nearby and to plan to spend the following day in prayer and fasting.

During their time of prayer and fasting, God revealed to them the reason for the resistance which they had encountered. A demonic principality of pride was reigning over the city of Cordoba. The only way this stronghold could be broken would be through a public display of its opposite—Christian humility.

The following day, Dawson and company went to the central mall shopping area in Cordoba and scattered themselves throughout the mall. They knelt with their faces to the cobblestones and began to earnestly pray that Jesus would be revealed to the city. Suddenly, the resistance was broken. Crowds of people began to gather around the missionaries to observe and hear what they had to say. People gladly received the gospel tracts and even asked that they first be autographed.

The receptivity of the shoppers became an open door for tremendous evangelism. Crowds gathered at the Plaza of St. Martin to listen as John Dawson preached the gospel to them. Many were so convicted by the Holy Spirit that they dropped to their knees and, in a flood of tears, repented of their sins as they received Christ as Savior.

It is to be noted that Dawson and his fellow missionaries could not effectively witness to God's kingdom in Cordoba simply by one-on-one witnessing and the distribution of gospel literature. It was only after they earnestly prayed for God's kingdom to come to Cordoba through a revelation of Jesus to the city that their efforts were successful. Their prayers focused upon the kingdom of God. The effect was that God instructed them and anointed them to be instrumental in bringing the kingdom to the lives of the people of Cordoba.

God wants us to pray the price for His kingdom to come and His will to be done in our lives, our families, our churches and our communities. But, so much of our praying is ineffective because we pray with the wrong focus. Our prayers for others may be focused upon the desire to see people live together in love and harmony and experience the blessings of productivity and prosperity. While these are admirable desires, they are not necessarily evidence of submission to God's kingdom rule. Therefore, such worthwhile desires are not to be the focus of our praying. We should pray rather that those for whom we petition will say yes to God's kingdom rule and allow the blessings of life to issue forth from His hand as tokens of His divine favor. We must be diligent and earnest in making the kingdom of God the focus of our praying.

Finally, if our prayers are to be salvaged from seduction, we need to understand the effect of prayer. If the focus of prayer is the kingdom of God, then the effect of prayer is personal submission to God's reign in our lives. If we are praying right, prayer will change us from being self-serving people to being true servants of God concerned with His interests.

It is easy to make ourselves—our needs and desires—the center of all our praying. But our praying is to be larger than ourselves. We must grasp the big picture. John Wesley said, "Thy kingdom come . . . is a prayer for that time when God will put an end to all misery, sin, infirmity, and death."(13) I would modify Wesley's statement to say that we are not simply praying for a *future* time when God will bring the woes of humanity to an end. We are praying that the kingdom of God would intervene in the lives of people *now* and put a stop to such works of the enemy. And as we pray for God's kingdom to come in the big picture, we will find that it will touch our lives and meet our needs as well. At the culmination of the very chapter in Matthew in which the Lord's Prayer is given, Jesus said, "Seek first [God's] kingdom and his righteousness, and all these things will be given to you as well" (6:33).

Our prayers will be salvaged from the danger of seduction as we learn to make God alone the object of our praying, the kingdom of God the focus of our praying and personal submission to God's kingdom reign the effect of our praying. This is the salvation of prayer.

Summing It Up

God wants each of us to examine our prayer lives. Are we praying with the heart, the will, the mind? Are we praying to God alone? Are our prayers preoccupied with the coming of God's kingdom and the effecting of His will? Are we submitting ourselves to His kingdom reign in our lives? If the answer to these questions is yes, then our prayer lives are spiritually potent and are a powerful instrument for the promotion of God's purposes. If the answer to these questions is no, then our prayer lives are spiritually sterile and cannot produce anything toward the promotion of God's kingdom.

I believe that God is calling us to pray the price to see His kingdom established in our lives, our families, our churches and our communities. If we will answer the call, we will learn firsthand the awesome power through prayer that Jesus has made available to us when He gave us His inspired outline of prayer in the Lord's Prayer.

Notes

1. John W. Whitehead, *The Stealing of America* (Westchester: Crossway Books, 1983), p. 47.

2. John Gage Allee, ed., *Webster's Encyclopedia of Dictionaries* (U.S.A.: Ottenheimer Publishers, Inc., 1958), p. 336.

3. From *The Gospel of Matthew* (Volume I: The Daily Study Bible Series) (Revised Edition), by William Barclay. Copyright © 1975 William Barclay. Used by permission of Westminster/John Knox Press and Saint Andrew Press, p. 194.

4. Ibid., p. 197.

5. Ibid., p. 192.

6. Ibid., p. 192f.

7. R. T. France, *Matthew* (Leicester and Grand Rapids: InterVarsity Press and William B. Eerdmans Publishing Company, 1985), p. 132.

8. Reprinted from *The Bible Exposition Commentary* Vol. 1 by Warren W. Wiersbe, published by Victor Books,

Copyright © 1989, SP Publications, Inc., Wheaton, IL 60187, p. 26.

9. Allee, p. 329.

10. France, p. 132.

11. Wiersbe, p. 26.

12. Reprinted with permission from *Charisma*, 600 Rinehart Road, Lake Mary, Florida 32746. Copyright April 1990, Strang Communications Company, pp. 47-48.

13. John Wesley, *The Nature of the Kingdom*, Edited and updated by Clare George Weakley, Jr. (Minneapolis: Bethany House Publishers, 1979), p. 157.

Chapter Two

The Rationale For Prayer

Andrew Murray tells of two men who were members of the New York Presbytery of the Dutch Reformed Church in the late nineteenth century. These men were so intent on seeing revival come to their presbytery that they called a meeting of all the clergymen under their jurisdiction to share the vision with them. In this meeting, the two presbyters discussed the importance of prayer and called for a show of hands indicating how much time each day the clergymen present spent in prayer to God for His blessing upon their ministries. The findings were staggering. One clergyman prayed only as much as thirty minutes per day. Only half prayed as much as fifteen minutes per day. All said they prayed at least five minutes per day, though one said later that he was not sure he spent even five minutes in daily prayer. The presbyter chairing the meeting exclaimed: "Prayer, the working power of the Church of Christ, and half of the workers make hardly any use of it!"(1)

The sin of prayerlessness results from unbelief and ignorance. First, prayerlessness results from unbelief. If people don't believe that their prayers will have any effect, they won't bother to pray. Second, prayerlessness results from ignorance. If people don't know how to pray correctly, then their prayers will be ineffective. Consequently, they will stop praying.

Jesus was concerned about the sin of prayerlessness. We've seen that His teaching aimed to save the spiritual discipline of prayer from those seductive forces at work in the religious world that would sterilize prayer and make the prayer lives of God's people ineffective. He realized that people discouraged by the ineffectiveness of their prayer lives would the more easily fall into the sin of prayerlessness. But Jesus was a pragmatist. He knew that people in danger of losing a sense of the value of prayer needed more than simply a snapshot analysis comparing misdirected praying with properly focused praying. If people's prayer lives are to be transformed, they must be delivered from the unbelief and ignorance that would ultimately lead to prayerlessness.

Jesus dealt with the unbelief that leads to prayerlessness through the vehicle of *inspiration*. His teachings *inspire* us to pray by imparting to us an understanding of the genuine value that prayer will have in our lives. Jesus dealt with the ignorance that leads to prayerlessness through the vehicle of *information*. His teachings *inform* us in our praying by giving us specific instructions in prayer that will assure us an effective prayer life. In so inspiring us to pray and informing us in our praying, we might say that Jesus provides us with a rationale for prayer.

This chapter is entitled "The Rationale For Prayer." What is a rationale? It is two things at once. First, it is "a logical basis" for an activity.(2) Second, it is an "exposition of principles" that provide guidance in an activity.(3) In talking about the rationale for prayer, we will look to Jesus' teaching in the Lord's Prayer and its context to determine the logical basis for prayer and the principles that govern prayer. We will do so by addressing two questions: First, why should we pray? Second, how should we pray?

Why Should We Pray?

The first aspect of the rationale for prayer is the logical basis for prayer. We will discuss the logical basis for prayer by addressing a question of purpose: Why should we pray? We must know the purpose that God intended for prayer to serve in our lives if we are to rightly understand and properly practice prayer.

As we inquire into the purpose for prayer, we must make sure at the outset that we inquire with the right motive if we expect to receive the right answer. Many people ask, "Why should we pray?" Some ask this question in unbelief. They do not believe that God hears or answers prayer. Therefore, they see no reason to pray. Others ask this question in exasperation. They feel that they have prayed in earnest without effectiveness. Therefore, they see no reason to continue praying. Still others ask this question with an eagerness to learn. They have experienced the joy of answered prayer and have begun to cultivate a consistent prayer life. They just want to learn more precisely the purpose of prayer in God's overall plan.

If we approach the subject of the purpose of prayer with the unbelief of the skeptic or the exasperation of the burn-out, we are not likely to be open-minded to the answer that comes to us through the teachings of Jesus. But if we are willing to "receive with meekness the engrafted word . . . " (James 1:21,KJV), then we will have no difficulty understanding God's purpose for our prayer lives.

Why should we pray? The purpose of prayer can be identified through examining the effects of prayers that are properly focused. We pointed out in our last chapter that prayers properly focused upon the kingdom of God will produce personal submission to God's reign in our lives. If personal submission to God's reign is the effect of godly prayer, then we may confidently suggest two reasons for prayer. First, we should pray in order that God's will be done *in* us. Second, we should pray in order that God's will be done *through* us. Let's consider these two reasons for prayer.

First of all, we should pray in order that God's will be done in us. We see this to be the case as we interpret the Lord's Prayer in the light of its immediate context in Matthew's gospel.

We learn from Matthew's gospel that the Lord's Prayer is a part of the Sermon on the Mount. As we stated in our last chapter, the Sermon on the Mount has been referred to as the Law of the Kingdom. As such, it sets forth God's laws governing the lives of those who by faith become citizens of God's kingdom. It has been observed by many New Testament expositors that these laws both show us what God's will is for our lives and expose our moral ineptitude, which prevents us from being able to keep God's laws and so conform to His will. We can render an *external obedience* to God's laws by refraining from such sins as murder, adultery, divorce, swearing and seeking revenge upon our enemies—sins that the Sermon on the Mount deals with explicitly. But our moral ineptitude prevents us from rendering an *internal obedience* to God's laws by refraining from the desire to commit such sins. Yet it is precisely this internal conformity to God's will that the Law of the Kingdom requires of us. We are capable in our own strength of doing God's will *for* us but not of allowing God's will to be done *in* us.

If our moral ineptitude prevents us from rendering an inward conformity to God's will, then how is the will of God to be done in us? The power to inwardly conform to God's will comes to us only in answer to our prayers. We must pray in order that God's will be done in us because personal submission to God's reign in our lives is the effect of prayer that is properly focused upon the kingdom of God. This is why Jesus taught us to pray, saying, "Your kingdom come, your will be done on earth as it is in heaven" (Matthew 6:10). Jesus realized that people could not render an *inward obedience* to the laws of God's kingdom until they had an *inward experience* of the reality of God's kingdom. For the presence of God's kingdom in the heart produces the righteousness of God's kingdom in the inner life.

We must pray in order that God's will be done *in* us. What is God's will for our inner life? It is righteousness for our spirits, peace for our minds and health for our bodies. These are not assets to be gained through human wisdom, skill or ability cooperating to produce the good life.

They are, rather, the fruits of believing prayer. We must look to God prayerfully in humility and in faith to receive "everything we need for life and godliness . . ." (2 Peter 1:3).

The value of prayer as the means of receiving the grace by which God's will is done in our spirits, minds and bodies is beautifully illustrated by the testimony of Linda Tyrrell of New Jersey who found hope for her life through the prayer ministry of "The 700 Club."(4) I give her story to illustrate just how prayer can override our own ineptitude as well as the best of the wisdom and skill of humankind and provide the divine means by which God's will is done in us.

Linda Tyrrell experienced a traumatic divorce that resulted in her developing agoraphobia—a fear of open places. Her condition worsened over the next four and a half years to the point that she could not leave the house without such symptoms of panic as a pounding heart, shortness of breath and shakiness all over. She became depressed, angry, resentful and bitter. She found herself dependent upon tranquilizers, anti-depressants, liquor and cigarettes to steady her nerves. She was regularly seeing a psychiatrist and two psychologists and attending a therapy group. Still, she experienced no marked improvement.

One day, Tyrrell was watching "The 700 Club" and decided to call the C.B.N. counseling center. She received biblical counseling and prayer. As she felt a tingling manifestation of the Holy Spirit's presence inundate her body, she experienced a release from the abnormal fears, the chemical dependencies and the inner vices of anger, resentment and bitterness. She experienced an inflow of love and peace that she could scarcely describe.

Tyrrell at once began to change her activities so that she is now constantly on the go. She now spends lots of time visiting people in nursing homes, attending church and participating in home fellowship groups. She has become very outgoing in mingling with people and helping them.

Tyrrell's testimony illustrates the role of prayer in bringing God's kingdom into our lives with the effect that God's will is done in us. God's will is trust—not fear; it is peace—not depression, anger and resentment; it is wholeness—not a life that is falling apart. Human willpower is not sufficient to change these negatives into positives. If it were, Tyrrell would certainly have resolved to be a happy peaceful person in her own strength. But prayer made the difference for Tyrrell. Through prayer, she in essence welcomed God's kingdom reign in her life. The result was that God's will was done in her.

Make no mistake about it. Unless we petition for it in our prayers, God's kingdom reign will not be established in our lives. Consequently, we will not be able to render an inward obedience to the Law of the Kingdom. But if we will faithfully pray that God's kingdom be sovereignly enthroned in our hearts, we will experience God's transforming grace bringing to our inner lives righteousness, peace, harmony and wholeness. We should pray in order that God's will be done *in* us.

Second, we should pray in order that God's will be done *through* us. We see this to be the case as we interpret the Lord's Prayer in the light of its immediate context in Luke's gospel.

Luke presents the Lord's Prayer in chapter 11 of his gospel. Though Luke is vague as to the setting in which Jesus taught His disciples to pray the Lord's Prayer, his placement of the prayer in his gospel immediately after the events of chapter 10 provides us a context in which to understand the prayer.

In Luke chapter 10, Jesus instructed His disciples to pray that God would send out laborers to bring a harvest of souls into His kingdom. Jesus then instructed them to go out in pairs to the various towns, preaching the gospel of the kingdom and healing the sick. Immediately after this narrative, Luke presents the parable of the Good Samaritan to illustrate the point that true piety is demonstrated through having compassion upon the hurting and ministering to their needs. From this snapshot analysis of the greater part of the chapter, two important insights emerge. First, we must ask God to send out workers to transact His kingdom business. Second, we must go out ourselves as God's workers to witness to the presence of His kingdom, to heal the sick and to minister in compassion to the needs of the hurting.

It is against this background that we find Luke reporting the occasion of Jesus' teaching His disciples the Lord's Prayer. In the context of Luke's gospel, we pray, "Your kingdom come" so that God will come and empower us to do His will in the world through sharing the gospel, healing the sick and ministering in divine compassion to the needs of the hurting. Why should we pray? We should pray that God's will might be done *through* us.

We saw earlier that God's will is not done *in* us by the strength of our own will power but only by the grace of

God given to us in answer to our prayers. We must be equally clear on the fact that God's will is not done *through* us by means of our own wisdom or ability but only by the grace of God given through us to others in answer to our prayers for them. While it is true that Christians should be actively involved in serving others in love, we must never forget that the most effective way in which we can serve others is to pray for them.

Kenneth Hagin tells of a Christian psychiatrist who learned this lesson in a remarkable way.(5) This Spirit-filled psychiatrist donated time working in the psychiatric wards of charity hospitals. In one hospital, he decided to experiment on a patient by treating him through prayer.

The patient in question had not spoken a word in three years. He sat still, glibly staring at the wall. The psychiatrist laid hands on him every day and said, "If there are evil spirits here, I rebuke them and command every one of them to leave in the name of the Lord Jesus Christ." He also spent five minutes each day praying over the patient in tongues—audibly if they were alone and silently if there were others nearby who might not understand.

Ten days after the psychiatrist started this treatment, the patient was talking. Within thirty days, he was sent home as completely cured. This psychiatrist has learned that prayer paves the way for God to minister grace through him to transform the lives of other people.

How many times have we felt powerless to help depressed, miserable people find peace and happiness! How often have we wished that we could help the suffering and diseased find relief from pain and healing for their bodies? We have fund-raisers to support medical research to advance our understanding of human psychology and physiology so that more people may find the good life. While all of these efforts are commendable, we must remember that God does not accomplish His will through us primarily through human wisdom, skill and ability. Rather, it is in answer to our prayers for others that He pours His grace and power through us to touch and transform the lives of others. Why should we pray? We should pray that God's will be done through us.

How Should We Pray?

We've discussed the first aspect of the rationale for prayer, i.e. its logical basis, by discussing a question of purpose: Why should we pray? We turn now to consider the second aspect of the rationale for prayer, i.e. the principles that govern prayer. We will do so by addressing a question of method: How should we pray? Our purpose isn't to delve into the specifics of the method for prayer laid out in the petitions of the Lord's Prayer. We will take up the text of the Lord's Prayer itself in later chapters. This chapter will point out the general characteristics of the method of prayer which Jesus taught as we examine the context of the Lord's Prayer in Matthew and Luke.

How should we pray? Jesus would answer that our method for prayer should be characterized by precision, persistence and prioritization. We will consider each of these characteristics in turn.

First of all, our prayers should be characterized by precision. That is to say, our prayers should not lack focus but should be specific. We read, "And when you pray, do not keep on babbling like pagans, for they think they will be heard because of their many words. Do not be like them, for your Father knows what you need before you ask him" (Matthew 6:7,8). We have already seen that these verses aim primarily at correcting a misconception held by pagans or Gentiles according to which repetition of certain potent words or phrases in prayer would guarantee the desired result. Though this is the primary concern that Jesus addressed in these verses, He also implied we do not need to make a case before God to convince Him to grant the petitions desired. Since God knows our needs before we ask Him, we can and should be specific in our petitions to Him.

Precision in prayer is characteristic of Jesus' teaching on prayer elsewhere in the Sermon on the Mount. Jesus presented these pertinent words: "Which of you, if his son asks for bread, will give him a stone? Or if he asks for a fish, will give him a snake? If you, then, though you are evil, know how to give good gifts to your children, how much more will your Father in heaven give good gifts to those who ask him! " (Matthew 7: 9-11). These verses show that God wants us to ask Him for the things that we desire, and He wants us to be specific in the asking. Our prayers are to be characterized by precision.

A humorous and potentially provocative illustration of this point is related by Paul Yonggi Cho, pastor of the world's largest Church—the Yoido Full Gospel Central Church in Seoul, Korea.(6) Cho began his ministry in a slum where he busied himself with one-on-one witnessing from door-to-door and preaching to a poverty-stricken congregation. He lived in a small room with no furniture and subsisted on very little income. He ate, studied and slept on the floor and walked many miles daily to carry out his visitation responsibilities.

One day, Cho's Bible reading impressed him with his standing as a child of the King of kings who is given privileges through Jesus' name to request and receive anything he needed. So he prayerfully petitioned God for a desk, a chair and a bicycle. Then he thanked God for them and closed his prayer with worship.

Cho patiently and faithfully waited for his desk, chair and bicycle to come. But six months passed with no answer. One evening, Cho was tired, hungry and discouraged. In exasperation, he complained to God that his prayer had not been answered. He had not received the things he had requested. Despairing of how he could teach others faith when his own prayers weren't being answered, Cho began to weep.

Suddenly, Cho began to feel very tranquil as the presence of the Lord came to him. He paused quietly as he knew God was getting ready to speak to him. The Holy Spirit said to him, "My son, I heard your prayer a long time ago." Cho blurted out, "Then where are my desk, chair and bicycle?" The Lord replied, "Yes, that is the trouble with you, and with all My children. They beg Me, demanding every kind of request, but they ask in such vague terms that I can't answer. Don't you know that there are dozens of kinds of desks, chairs and bicycles? But you've simply asked Me for a desk, chair and bicycle. You never ordered a specific desk, chair or bicycle."

Cho immediately asked God to cancel all his prayers for these items, and he offered a new prayer. He prayerfully specified the dimensions of the desk and requested that it be made of Philippine mahogany. The chair was to have an iron frame with wheels so that he could roll around and act like a big shot. The bicycle was to be American-made with gears for regulating speed. His prayer was very precise.

In a short time, God provided Cho with all of these things. He had a Philippine mahogany desk, an iron framed rolling chair manufactured by Mitsubishi and a slightly used American-made bicycle with gears which was passed on to him from an American missionary's son.

Now, I said that this illustration is not only humorous but potentially provocative. I say this because many are critical of the idea of praying for things that we desire for our own benefit and pleasure. They are quick to quote such verses as this: "When you ask, you do not receive, because you ask with wrong motives, that you may spend what you get on your pleasures" (James 4:3). They reason that we are never to ask God for things that are for our personal pleasure. But the word which James uses for "pleasure" in this passage *(hedone)* is the Greek term from which we derive our English word "hedonist." A hedonist is one who lives solely for pleasure and, therefore, cares little for the welfare of others except as they contribute to his pleasure. James is not castigating prayer for the things that we desire. He is attacking selfish motives that give undue place to personal pleasure. His words do not conflict with those of Jesus who said, "Ask and you will receive, and your joy will be complete" (John 16:24).

Once we get past the erroneous belief that God desires to deprive us of the pleasures of life, then we will have no trouble praying with precision for the things that we desire. We will know that when we ask our Father for bread, He will not give us a stone; when we ask Him for a fish, He will not give us a snake. This assurance will lead us to believe that we will receive what we ask for. When we are convinced that God will grant our petitions, we will make our prayers very specific. Our prayers are to be characterized by precision.

Second, our prayers are to be characterized by persistence. Jesus intended for us to pray the petitions of the Lord's Prayer persistently until we receive everything for which we ask. We learn this from the context the Lord's Prayer in Luke's gospel.

In Luke's gospel, the Lord's Prayer is immediately followed by a parable that emphasizes persistence in petitioning for the meeting of one's needs. (See Luke 11:5-10.) Jesus tells of a man who received a guest at his house in the middle of the night. Not having food to set before his guest, he went to the home of a neighbor and began to knock on his door. Once the neighbor was awakened, the man requested three small loaves of bread with which to refresh his guest. The sluggish neighbor was quite unwilling to get up and answer the door. He yelled out, "Don't bother me. The door is already locked, and my children are with me in bed. I can't get up and give you anything" (vs. 7). Nonetheless, the man continued to knock. He would not take no for an answer. Jesus commended this persistence. He said, "I tell you, though he will not get up and give him the bread because he is his friend, yet because of the man's boldness he will get up and give him as much as he needs" (vs. 8).

Jesus told this parable about persistence in petitioning for the meeting of one's needs right after He gave the disciples the Lord's Prayer. But then, to make sure they got the point, He followed the parable with more teaching on the need to be persistent in prayer. He said, "Ask and it will be given to you; seek and you will find; knock and the door will be opened to you. For everyone who asks receives; he who seeks finds; and to him who knocks, the door will be opened" (vs. 9, 10). The verbs in these verses are present tense imperatives which, in New Testament Greek, call for continuous action. Jesus encouraged His disciples to persist in their asking, seeking and knocking until they receive the answer to their prayers. Our prayers are to be characterized by persistence.

Many Christians object to this point. They maintain that persistence in prayers of petition indicates a lack of faith. If we truly pray in faith, they say, we will simply make our request of God, believe that He hears and answers our prayer, give thanks for the answer and leave the matter entirely in God's hands. This practice does have scriptural merit. (See Mark 11:24; Philippians 4:6,7.) It has its proper place in prayer. But our present discussion has shown us sufficient biblical basis for prayers of persistence. Scripture exhorts us to offer prayers of petition with persistence until we receive tangible evidence that the answer to our prayers has been granted.

Persistence in prayer does not reveal a lack of faith. To the contrary! It may reveal relentless faith. A case in point comes to us through the testimony of Frederick K. C. Price. Before Price became a Christian, he developed a small growth on one side of his chest. He went to the doctor to have it checked. It was examined, declared benign and surgically removed. Sometime after becoming a Christian and becoming acquainted with the teaching of the New Testament concerning faith and healing, Price developed a similar growth on the other side of his chest. He decided that this time he would believe God for healing and would not go to the doctor. (While I do not recommend this course of action for everyone, this is what Price was prepared to do.)

Price claimed Mark 11:24, which reads, "Therefore I tell you, whatever you ask for in prayer, believe that you have received it, and it will be yours." On the basis on this verse, he prayed for his healing and declared in faith, "I believe that I have received my healing." Every morning, he would look at the growth in the mirror and boldly declare, "I believe that I have received my healing." Nonetheless, the growth continued to get bigger until it was as large as a silver dollar. It pained him so badly that Price says he couldn't bear to touch it while showering. Still, Price was relentless in confessing his healing. After nine months of such persistence, Price looked in the mirror one morning to find that the growth had vanished overnight.

This illustration is especially illuminating because it suggests not so much a dichotomy as a relationship between the prayer of faith and persistence in prayer. Technically, we would have to say that Price prayed one prayer of faith for his healing and then persisted in a daily confession of faith affirming his healing. But Price's daily confession of faith, while not formulated as a prayer, amounts to a daily prayer of thanksgiving in which Price persisted until the healing materialized. Viewed from this perspective, we would be obliged to conclude that Price persisted in faith and in prayer until he obtained tangible evidence of the answer to his prayer.

We must also pray and believe with persistence. We must rid ourselves of the thought that praying about a matter repeatedly is a sign of unbelief or weak faith. Quite to the contrary, persistence in believing prayer can and should be a sign of relentless faith that will not give up until the answer to prayer materializes. Jesus taught that prayer must be characterized by persistence.

Finally, prayer must be characterized by prioritization. In our prayer lives, we are to put first things first. This point is communicated to us through the Lord's Prayer in two ways. It is communicated through the structure of the prayer and through the focus of the prayer.

First of all, the structure of the Lord's Prayer suggests to us that prayer is to be characterized by prioritization. The prayer has a three-part structure. It begins with a statement of address to God, it continues with six petitions presented to God and it closes with a doxology in praise of God. It is important to note the prioritization of the six petitions. The first three petitions concern God and His glory. They worship God, call for the coming of His kingdom to the earth and request the establishment of His will in the earth. The last three petitions concern man and his needs. They request physical nourishment, spiritual purgation and divine protection. By way of the ordering of these petitions, we learn that our concern in prayer should always be to give glory to God first before we petition for the meeting of our needs. This is the prioritization of prayer.

It is not only the structure of the Lord's Prayer but also its focus that impresses upon us the need for our prayers to be characterized by prioritization. The focus of the Lord's Prayer is, from beginning to end, the kingdom of God. Thus Jesus is teaching us that we are to aim at glorifying God through prayer in every petition of prayer—even those petitions that request the supplying of our personal needs. When we request of God things that we need, we are to request them primarily for God's glory and only secondarily for our personal benefit.

Do you need a job or extra income? Request it of God so that you can glorify God through your performance on the job and through your use of the extra income. Do you need a new car? Request it of God so that you can glorify God by using the car to serve God by serving others. Do you need healing in your body? Request it of God so that you will have more strength and vigor with which to worship God and serve others. No matter what you need from God, always request it with a view to using the answer for the furtherance of God's glory. This is the prioritization of prayer.

Summing It Up

In giving us a rationale for prayer, Jesus inspires us to pray and instructs us in our praying. He inspires us to pray with the assurance that prayer, and prayer alone, will result in God's will being done in us and through us. He instructs us in our praying by the exhortations to pray with precision, with persistence and with prioritization.

As we heed God's word to us, we will find that our prayer lives become rich and rewarding. Our wills will be conformed to God's will and our prayers will be answered. Thus our prayers will have the effect of establishing God's kingdom both in our lives and in our world. This is what prayer is all about. And this is the goal of Jesus' teaching on prayer that comes to us through a study of the context of the Lord's Prayer.

Notes

1. Andrew Murray, *The Prayer Life* (Springdale, Pennsylvania: Whitaker House, 1981), p. 18.

2. John Gage Allee, ed., *Webster's Encyclopedia of Dictionaries* (U.S.A.: Ottenheimer Publishers, Inc., 1958), p. 305.

3. Ibid.

4. Pat Robertson and William Proctor, *Beyond Reason: How Miracles Can Change Your Life* (New York: Bantam Books, 1984), pp. 116ff.

5. Kenneth E. Hagin, *The Believer's Authority*, Second edition (Tulsa: Faith Library Publication, 1984), p. 65.

6. Paul Yonggi Cho, *The Fourth Dimension* (Plainfield, New Jersey: Logos International, 1979), pp. 10ff.

7. Frederick K. C. Price, *Is Healing For All?* (Tulsa: Harrison House, Inc., 1976), pp. 115-117.

PART TWO

The Center Of

The Lord's Prayer

Our Father in heaven,
hallowed be your name,
your kingdom come,
your will be done
on earth as it is in heaven.
(Matthew 6:9, 10)

Chapter Three

Prayer And The Keys

Our Father in heaven, hallowed be your name, ...
— Matthew 6:9b.

When I decided to embark upon the founding of the Sheepfold of Suffolk, Virginia—the independent charismatic church that I pastor at this writing—I encountered what I considered at the time to be unexpected opposition. I knew that God had called me into full-time ministry. I had prepared academically through college and seminary studies. As far as my resources would allow, I was going "by the book" in the initial stages of preparation for the planting of a local church. Yet dissenting voices began to come to the fore. A local pastor advised me to pick another city for my church-planting venture. A traveling evangelist informed me that God had told him I was not to start a church at all. Still another evangelist prophesied over me that I was called to personal, one-on-one ministry. I'm sure that each of these gentlemen was sincere and had my best interest at heart. But, listening to so many advisers began to dampen my zeal for ministry and had the effect of calling into question the affirmation of my own pastor whose leadership and sensitivity to the Holy Spirit I trusted.

Feeling somewhat pulled between my assurance of God's call and the conflicting voices of sincere advisors, I determined to set aside three hours one evening for prayer with the goal of "praying through" to a peaceful resolve. After getting home from work, cutting the grass and having dinner, I finally settled into prayer at 8:00 p.m. At about 10:30 p.m., I suddenly saw a vision of the hand of Jesus. With His index finger pointed slightly upward and the remaining three fingers folded over against the palm, He held a golden key that was poised heavenward. After the vision vanished, I prayed for wisdom concerning its meaning. In answer, God enlightened me to the fact that prayer moves the hand of Jesus to turn the key that unlocks heaven in order that we might live under an open heaven. As for the situation about which I was praying, I understood that prayer is the key to the knowledge of God's will for my life and to the resources necessary to carry out His will.

Sometime later, I was reflecting upon this vision and its meaning when I realized the connection that the Scripture makes between prayer and the keys of the kingdom of heaven. Jesus said to Peter, "I will give you the keys of the kingdom of heaven; whatever you bind on earth will be bound in heaven, and whatever you loose on earth will be loosed in heaven" (Matthew 16:19). In Matthew 18:18, Jesus delegated this same power of binding and loosing to all of His disciples and then went on to say in verse 19, "Again, I tell you that if two of you on earth agree about anything you ask for, it will be done for you by my Father in heaven." The keys of the kingdom of heaven are used for binding and loosing, and binding and loosing take place through prayer. Truly, prayer is a key that unlocks heaven's blessings upon us.

If prayer is a key to heaven's blessings, then certainly our Lord's inspired outline for prayer will impart to us such a key and will instruct us in how to use it. This is precisely what we find at the outset of the prayer. The opening address and the first petition read, "Our Father in heaven, hallowed be your name, . . ." (Matthew 6:9). As we will see, the hallowing of God's name in prayer is a key to knowing God, worshiping God and reaching the world for God.

Knowing God

Hallowing God's name requires the acknowledgment of His name. By acknowledging God's name, we come to know God. Thus the hallowing of God's name in prayer is a key to knowing God. Let's see just how this takes place.

In biblical times, the act of naming a child was a matter of greater significance than we treat it today. It was believed that a person's name communicated something of the person's nature and characteristics. The name even had some part to play in forecasting a person's future. A classic biblical example is found in the twin sons of Isaac and

Rebekah—namely, Jacob and Esau. (See Genesis 25:21-26.) Esau was born first. His body was red and hairy. He was named Esau—a name based upon the word in Hebrew for "hairy." He was also called Edom, which means "red." Jacob was born second with his hand grasping Esau's heel. He was named Jacob, which means "he grasps the heel"—a figurative way of saying "he deceives." Thus the names were based upon observable phenomena surrounding the twins' birth.

Yet the names were also significant because they communicated something of the character of the boys and provided an accurate forecasting of their future. Esau, or Edom, whose latter name means "red," sold his birthright as the firstborn son to his brother Jacob in exchange for a bowl of red stew. (See Genesis 25:29-34.) Jacob, whose name implies deception, used intrigue to steal from his brother both his birthright and the blessing of his father. (See Genesis 27:1-40.)

When we understand that names, in biblical times, communicated the nature and character of the one bearing the name, then we grasp the significance of Jesus' reference in the Lord's Prayer to God's name. In the words of D. F. Kelly, "God's name stood for God himself."(1) We conclude that to know God's name is to know God.

What is God's name? Jesus tells us that His name is, "Our Father in heaven." Some might object that this is a title and not a name. But in biblical thought, a fine line of distinction exits between a title and a name. For instance, Abraham's name was originally Abram, which means "exalted father." God later changed his name to the longer Abraham, which means "father of many." Now we would consider the designations "exalted father" and "father of many" to be titles and not names. Yet these titles were the names of the father of Israel.

Just as "exalted father" and "father of many" were the names of Israel's first patriarch, so "Our Father in heaven" is the name of our God. In this name, we find the summation of all that God is in relation to us. When we know Him by this name, we know Him in the truest sense. Let's consider this name of our God and see what we can learn from it.

Jesus taught us that God is "Our Father." Now the fatherhood of God speaks to us of the immanence of God. By that I mean that God becomes our Father when He comes to live in us by His Spirit. We see this point in the teaching of the New Testament concerning the new birth. We learn that we are born through the seed of God's Spirit into His family when we put our faith in the Lord Jesus Christ. (See John 1:12.) We also learn that through the new birth, God's Spirit comes to live in us. He is referred to as the "Spirit of sonship" and gives us the ability to address God as our "Father." (See Romans 8:15-18.)

God's fatherhood is within us. As such, it is synonymous with God's kingdom, which is within us. (See Luke 17:21.) Our Father is the King of all kings. We are children of royalty. As our Father, God gives us life, love, instruction, correction and provision while conforming us to His image. As our Father the King, God establishes His throne in us, writes His laws upon our hearts and minds and brings His kingdom to our lives, making us its faithful citizens.

Jesus taught us not only that God is our Father but that he is "Our Father *in heaven*." As our Father, He is immanent. That is, He lives within us. As our Father *in heaven,* He is transcendent. That is, He lives over us. For He is the Creator, Sustainer and Supreme Governor of all. His sovereign reign extends to the entire created order. This God who is over all is our Father. And as our Father, He employs His infinite resources of love, wisdom and power on our behalf.

To acknowledge God as "Our Father in heaven" is to find soul rest through our acceptance *with* Him and our security *through* Him. William Barclay recounts an old story dating back to the time of the Roman Empire that provides an apt analogy of the acceptance and security that the Christian experiences when he acknowledges God as his Father.(2) The story is about a Roman Emperor who had just won a great military victory. In typical Roman style, the Emperor and the Roman militia were marching through the streets of Rome with their prisoners of war in their train. The streets of the city were lined with ecstatic citizens celebrating Rome's latest victory. To keep order, there were legionaries on duty along the streets holding the people back in their places thus providing clear passageway for the victory march. As the Emperor's chariot came in sight of the platform from which the Empress and family were observing the processional, a little boy jumped from the platform and ran toward the chariot. Dodging the crowd, he attempted to pass through the legs of a legionary. The legionary swung his arms down, picked him up and said to him, "You can't do that, boy! Don't you know who that is in that chariot? That's the Emperor. You can't run out to his chariot." Looking down into the legionary's face, the little boy laughed and said, "He may be your Emperor, but he's my father." Barclay comments, "That is exactly the way the Christian feels toward God. The might, and the majesty, and the power are the might, and the majesty, and the power of one whom Jesus taught us to call *Our Father*."

Acknowledging God's name brings us to know Him not only as our Father but as our Lord. This also is His name. We learn this from the Old Testament account of the calling of Moses. When God called Moses to lead the people of Israel out of Egypt, Moses asked God, "Suppose I go to the Israelites and say to them, `The God of your fathers has sent me to you,' and they ask me, `What is his name?' Then what shall I tell them?" (Exodus 3:13). God responded, "I AM WHO I AM. This is what you are to say to the Israelites: `I AM has sent me to you' .... Say to the Israelites, `The Lord, the God of your fathers . . . has sent me to you'" (vs. 14,15). After Moses obeyed and went to Pharoah, God spoke again to Moses concerning His name. He said, "I appeared to Abraham, to Isaac and to Jacob as God Almighty, but by my name the Lord I did not make myself known to them" (Exodus 6:3).

What does it mean to know God as Lord? We immediately think of a lord as one who exercises authority over subjects. Thus God's lordship over us makes us think of our obligation as His subjects to submit to and obey Him. It is certainly important that we grasp this particular connotation of lordship. God expects His people to honor and obey Him. However, it is noteworthy that God communicated His lordship to the people of Israel through a series of "Lord names" indicating who He desires to be in relation to His people. Each of these names was given in a particular historical setting in which God was responding to a need of His people. The most fruitful study of these names would necessitate rehearsing bits of Israel's history leading up to the giving of each of these names. But, it will serve our purposes to show how God's revealed names respond to the needs of His people on each level of their existence.(3) Since God is not only Lord of Israel but Lord of the Church, we will show how these "Lord names" respond to our needs on every level of our existence—spirit, soul and body.

What are the needs of our spirits? We need to be cleansed from sin, made righteous and consecrated to God. God has responded to these needs by revealing Himself to us through two names. God's name is *Jehovah-tsidkenu*, or "The Lord Our Righteousness." He is also *Jehovah-m'kaddesh*, or "The Lord Who Sanctifies." As our righteousness and our sanctification, God is the source for the meeting of our spiritual needs.

What are the needs of our souls? We need peace for our minds, guidance for our wills and security for our emotions. God has responded to these needs by revealing Himself to us through three names. God is *Jehovah-shalom*, or "The Lord Is Peace." He is peace for our minds. God is *Jehovah-ra'ah*, or "The Lord Is My Shepherd". As our Shepherd, He provides guidance for our wills. God is *Jehovah-shammah*. This last name has two meanings. It means "The Lord Is There." It also means "The Lord Is The Overflowing One". It speaks of God's companionship with us which causes us to experience His divine fullness. God's companionship *with* us and His divine fullness *in* us provide security for our emotions. As our peace, our guidance and our security, God is the source for the meeting of the needs of our souls.

What are the needs of our bodies? We need provision, health and protection. God has responded to these needs by revealing Himself to us through three names. God is *Jehovah-jireh,* or "The Lord Will Provide." He provides for our physical needs. God is *Jehovah-rapha,* or "I, The Lord, Am Your Healer." He is the source of our health. God is *Jehovah-nissi,* or "The Lord Is My Banner." A banner is a military ensign, or standard, which speaks of defense. As the Lord our banner, God protects us from all harm. As our provider, our healer and our protector, God is the source for the meeting of the needs of our bodies.

When we understand that God's "Lord names" reveal who God desires to be in relation to us, then we realize that His names invite us to know Him. As we acknowledge each of God's names, we come to know Him as he reveals Himself through that name.

When we pray, we should acknowledge God's names in reference to our needs. Do we need deliverance from sinful habits? We should acknowledge God's name as "The Lord Our Righteousness" and "The Lord Our Sanctifier." Do we need healing for our bodies? We should acknowledge God's name as "The Lord Our Healer." Do we need work or extra income to pay bills? We should acknowledge God's name as "The Lord Our Provider." Are we lonely and troubled? We should acknowledge God's name as "The Lord Who Is There" and "The Lord Our Peace." Through thus acknowledging God's name in prayer in reference to our needs, we come to know God as the one who sets us above our circumstances. God's promise is, "I will set him on high, because he hath known my name" (Psalm 91:14,KJV).

Finally, acknowledging God's name brings us to know Him not only as our Father and our Lord but as our Savior. Jesus said of Himself, "I have come in my Father's name" (John 5:43). So then, to acknowledge God's name in prayer is to acknowledge the name of Jesus in prayer. The name Jesus means "The Lord Saves." When we acknowledge Jesus' name in prayer, we come to know the Lord as our Savior. The result is the experience of God's salvation.

The fact that acknowledging Jesus' name in prayer causes us to know God experientially as Savior is beautifully illustrated by an event from the life and ministry of Smith Wigglesworth.(4) Wigglesworth was in Wales once when he was asked to visit and pray for a bedfast man by the name of Lazarus. Lazarus was a minister who labored in the tin mines during the daytime and preached in the evenings. His constant labors took a toll on his body until he collapsed from exhaustion and became bedfast. He developed tuberculosis and lay helpless for six years. He couldn't even lift a spoon to his mouth.

When Wigglesworth arrived at Lazarus' home, he found that this man of God had become very bitter. He had been a faithful servant of the Lord. Yet God had allowed him to become helpless and bedfast. Furthermore, many people had prayed for him and God didn't seem to be answering prayer. Lazarus' bitterness had drained him of faith for healing.

Wigglesworth called upon the family of Lazarus to gather seven other believers to assist him in ministering to Lazurus. Once they were gathered, Wigglesworth had them encircle Lazarus' bed. He explained that they were not to pray. Rather, they were just to say the name of Jesus over and over again. The eight believers began whispering the name of Jesus repetitiously. As they did, the power of God fell and lifted five times. Then it fell a sixth time and remained.

Wigglesworth told Lazarus that God's power was present to heal him and that it was up to him to accept it. The man at once confessed that he had grown bitter against God and had grieved the Holy Spirit. With Wigglesworth's encouragement, the man repented of his bitterness and asked that he be healed for the glory of God. At once, power went through Lazarus' body and he was healed. He got out of bed unassisted, dressed himself and went walking down the stairs as everyone together sang the doxology. When word spread that Lazarus had been raised up, people came from near and far to hear his testimony with the result that many were saved.

Notice that Wigglesworth and those assisting him in ministry in this incident did not pray per se. They simply spoke the name of Jesus. Every time they said the name of Jesus, they were saying the equivalent of "The Lord saves, the Lord saves." The result was that the Lord saved Lazarus through raising him up from the bed of affliction and saved many souls through the word of his testimony.

When we acknowledge the name of Jesus in prayer, we are acknowledging God as our Savior. This does not just mean that we are acknowledging His grace in the forgiveness of our sins. The biblical concept of salvation is holistic. It applies not only to the spirit but also to the soul and the body. To call upon God as our Savior is to receive from His grace wholeness for the totality of our being.

We've seen that hallowing God's name requires the acknowledgment of His name. In acknowledging God's name we come to know Him. We know Him as our heavenly Father, our Lord and our Savior. But hallowing God's name in prayer is not only the key to knowing God. It is also the key to worshiping Him.

Worshiping God

Hallowing God's name must begin with the acknowledgment of His name. But there is more involved in hallowing a name than merely acknowledging it. To hallow means to sanctify. It is through the sanctification of God's name that we worship God.

To hallow God's name is to sanctify His name. In the Lord's Prayer from both Matthew and Luke, Jesus speaks of hallowing God's name. (See Matthew 6:9; Luke 11:2.) These are the only two places in the New Testament where the term that Jesus used here (*hagiazo*) is translated "hallow." This same term is used in twenty-six other New Testament passages where it is rendered "sanctify."(5) We worship God when we hallow His name by sanctifying His name in our hearts.

What does it mean to "hallow" or "sanctify"? Basically, it means removing something from the category of the common and placing it in the category of the hcly. In applying this definition to specific things or persons, the Scripture identifies three implications of the term—distinction, dedication and devotion.

First of all, sanctification speaks of distinction. This is the meaning implied in Jesus' statements that the Temple sanctifies the gold of the Temple (see Matthew 23:17), and the altar sanctifies the gift on the altar. (See Matthew 23:19.) That is, the gold used in the construction of the Temple is distinct from all other gold in that it is set apart for God. Likewise, the animal sacrificed upon the altar is distinct from other animals in that it is set apart for God. In these instances, the gold of the Temple and the animal upon the altar are sanctified.

Second, sanctification speaks of dedication. The epistles imply that the people of God are sanctified by the blood of Christ (see Hebrews 13:12), by the Word of God (see Ephesians 5:26) and by the Holy Spirit. (See Romans 15:16.) Through the blood, the Word and the Spirit, people are called upon and enabled to dedicate their lives no longer to the service of sin but to the service of God. Those so dedicated to God are sanctified.

Third, sanctification speaks of devotion. This is the meaning implied in the words of the Apostle Peter who encouraged believers to sanctify God in their hearts (1 Peter 3:15). When our hearts are so completely devoted to God that we do His bidding willingly and joyfully, we sanctify God.

Now that we understand what it means to "hallow" or "sanctify" something or someone as these terms are used in the New Testament, let's ask the question that will make these insights relevant to our understanding of the Lord's Prayer. What does it mean to "hallow" or "sanctify" God's name? We will suggest two answers. First, it is to acknowledge God in His holiness as distinct from all others and, therefore, to be revered. Second, it is to acknowledge God as worthy of our dedication and devotion and, therefore, to be adored. To hallow God's name is to revere and adore Him. Such reverence and adoration are the substance of worship.

It is important that we know how to worship God in the right way. Jesus said, "God is spirit, and his worshipers must worship in spirit and in truth" (John 4:24). Genuine worship arises from an individual's spirit and must be offered with sincerity. It is with our hearts that we must reverence and adore our God.

I wonder just how much we understand worship today. We often hear "full gospel" people criticize mainline denominational churches for their "dead services." In place of their dead services, we have live services replete with singing, clapping, dancing and shouting. We pride ourselves on the fact that we really know how to worship God. But do we? Does our worship demonstrate reverence for God and adoration of God? If not, we aren't really worshiping Him.

I vividly remember a particular worship service that I attended while I was in my teens in which God dealt with me about the sincerity of my worship. The service was in the church where I had received the baptism of the Holy Spirit not long before. Though it was a small church, it was one of those that did not believe in "dead services." But on this particular night, we were singing a hymn when my mind began to drift into never-never land. Suddenly, the Holy Spirit nudged me back to attention. It was as if the Lord were saying to me, "How can you be worshiping Me in song when you are thinking neither about the song nor about Me?" I remember how I responded at once to God's rebuke. I winced as I realized He was right. Then

I extended my hands heavenward, focused my mind upon the words of praise that I was singing and opened my heart to God. As I did, God poured His Spirit into me in a tangible way. Over the next few seconds, I literally felt myself getting fuller and fuller from my stomach up. My delight was increasing in direct proportion to the divine fullness. I thought to myself, If it gets any better, I don't know what I'm going to do! I felt as though I were going to explode with joy. Then suddenly, the fullness of the Spirit reached the top of my head and overflowed me. I use the word "overflowed" intentionally as I felt my face being bathed in God's Spirit. Then the sensations subsided. God had richly rewarded my submission to His rebuke and my responsiveness.

I relate this experience to emphasize the inwardness of worship. You can be in a live worship service replete with singing, clapping, dancing and shouting and still not be worshiping God from within. To worship God, you must open your heart to Him in reverence and adoration.

We can learn much about worship from the Old Testament. It is significant that when God sent Moses to Pharaoh, He sent him with the message, "Let my people go, so that they may worship me in the desert" (Exodus 7:16). Judging from this statement, we would expect to find that God would, upon leading Israel through the Red Sea and into the desert, teach His people to worship Him. And that He did. He taught His people both to revere Him and to adore Him.

First, God taught the people of Israel in the wilderness to revere Him. When Moses and the congregation of Israel reached the wilderness of Sinai, God instructed Moses to have the people wash their clothes and abstain from sexual relations for three days so as to consecrate themselves. At the end of the three days, they appeared before God at Mount Sinai where God spoke to Moses in their hearing. God told Moses to set up borders around the mountain so that nobody would attempt to climb up the mountain to see God. Anyone who dared to break through these borders was to be executed.

At the appointed time, Moses and all of Israel gathered at the foot of the mountain. Suddenly, thunder, lightning and a loud trumpet blast occurred as God descended upon the mountain in thick smoke. The mountain began to quake, and the people began to shake with fear. They listened as God summoned Moses up the mountain and gave to him the Ten Commandments. When it was all over, the people said to Moses, "Speak to us yourself and we will listen. But do not have God speak to us or we will die" (Exodus 20:19).

Why did God reveal Himself to Israel in such a way as to move them to fear and trembling? Moses answers this question for us. He said to the people, "Do not be afraid. God has come to test you, so that the fear of God will be with you to keep you from sinning" (Exodus 20:20). God was teaching the people to revere Him. This is the first component of worship.

Second, God taught the people of Israel in the wilderness to adore Him. God came to Moses on another occasion and revealed His glory to Moses. God put Moses in a mountain cleft, covered Moses with His hand and passed by. He removed His hand so that Moses could see the backside of God. As Moses looked upon God's glory, the Lord proclaimed these words of self-revelation:

> The Lord, the Lord, the compassionate and gracious God, slow to anger, abounding in love and faithfulness, maintaining love to thousands, and forgiving wickedness, rebellion and sin. Yet he does not leave the guilty unpunished; he punishes the children and their children for the sin of the fathers to the third and fourth generation—Exodus 34:6,7.

You can just imagine the effect it must have had upon the people of Israel when Moses told them about God's glory and the accompanying words of God's self-revelation. The God that they had learned to fear was not a tyrant. God is just, yes. But He is also a gracious, compassionate, merciful and faithful God. Such a revelation must have moved them to deep adoration as they realized that this God of such awesome power loved them and desired to bless them. In so learning to adore Him, they learned the second component of worship.

As hallowing God's name in prayer is a key to worship, so worshiping God is a key to living under an open heaven and receiving the blessings of God. This point is beautifully confirmed by Everett L. Fullam, rector of St. Paul's Episcopal Church of Darien, Connecticut.(6) Fullam tells of a woman who visited a well-attended Tuesday morning service at his church. She felt so well received that she took the liberty to share with those present an urgent prayer concern. Her husband had a rare leg disease.

The doctor had given him up to die. The woman requested prayer for him.

Fullam led those present into hallowing God's name through worship and praise. They then proceeded into prayer, asking God to heal the man.

A week later, the woman came back and reported that the doctor was planning to amputate her husband's legs as he now felt that it was possible to save his life. She requested continued prayer. Fullam again led the people before God as they, in his words, "worshiped and praised and prayed some more." They again prayed for the man to be healed.

The next week, the woman returned with a victory report. Since the doctor had already planned to amputate the man's legs, he made the decision to try an unusual treatment first with the slim hope that the man's legs might be saved. Incisions were made on both legs all the way from the hip to the ankle. The following day, the doctor came in to inspect the bandages. He discovered to the surprise and joy of all that the legs were totally healed! Even the doctor recognized the healing as miraculous.

God is looking for those who sincerely worship Him so that He can bless them. The Bible says, "For the eyes of the Lord run to and fro throughout the whole earth, to shew himself strong in the behalf of them whose heart is perfect toward him" (2 Chronicles 16:9,KJV). In what sense are our hearts to be perfect toward God? They are to be sincerely devoted to Him. Sincere devotion to God is reflected in genuine worship of God. It must be from our hearts that we reverence and adore Him. Through such reverence and adoration, we hallow His name.

Reaching The World For God

Hallowing God's name is not only the key to knowing and worshiping God, it is also the key to reaching the world for God. We've seen that hallowing God's name through *acknowledging* it is the key to the knowledge of God. We've seen also that hallowing God's name through *sanctifying* it is the key to the worship of God. We now point out that hallowing God's name through *declaring* it is the key to reaching the world for God.

John Wesley said that to pray that God's name be hallowed is to pray that God be known.(8) We've already seen that our hallowing of God's name in prayer brings us to know God. But we would be remiss if we failed to point out that our hallowing of God's name in prayer is a key to bringing others to know God. For when we know God, our lives become a declaration of God's name to others so that they too can come to know Him.

How does the hallowing of God's name become a key to reaching the world for God? There are two steps in the progression. First, hallowing God's name becomes the key to the unity of believers. Second, the unity of believers is the key to the evangelization of the world.

First of all, the hallowing of God's name produces the unity of believers. In the prayer of intercession, Jesus prayed these words for His disciples: "Holy Father, protect them by the power of your name—the name you gave me—so that they may be one as we are one" (John 17:11). What is the name that God gave to Jesus? The angel of God announced to His mother Mary, " . . . you are to give him the name Jesus, because he will save his people from their sins" (Matthew 1:21). As we have seen, Jesus means "the Lord saves." As we hallow God's name as the Lord who saves, we experience God's salvation with the result that we become one with the people of God.

God intends for His people to live together in unity. God communicated this to the family of the Sheepfold in a creative way. My aunt Sarah was ill one Sunday morning and couldn't make it to church. After the service, a couple of brothers from the church went with me to visit her and pray for her. As we stood around her bed with hands clasped together in prayer, Sarah and the two brothers began to see different aspects of a single vision. They saw our small group from the Sheepfold walking together to a nearby lake. Then they saw the group walk into the waters and submit themselves to a corporate baptism. While they were seeing the vision, I was praying in tongues.

When we finished our visit one of the brothers asked me if I knew any Spanish. I said that I had studied Spanish on my own for a few weeks some time ago but hadn't gotten very far before I gave it up. When I inquired why he had asked, he said to me, "While you were praying in tongues over Sarah's bed, I heard you say three times the Spanish words meaning `one heart.'"

Through the vision of the corporate baptism and the message calling us to one heart, God was seeking to communicate to us the importance of unity among His people in the Sheepfold. His message to us was the same as the Apostle Paul's inspired word to the Christians of the church in Corinth. Paul wrote, "I appeal to you, brothers, in the name of the Lord Jesus Christ, that all of you agree with one another so that there may be no divisions among

you and that you may be perfectly united in mind and in thought" (1 Corinthians 1:10).

Why is God so concerned about the unity of believers? He is concerned that His people be one because the unity of believers is the key to the evangelization of the world. Jesus prayed in the prayer of intercession that God's name would protect and unify His people for the purpose of effectively reaching the world with the message of God's love. Jesus prayed, "May they be brought to complete unity to let the world know that you sent me and have loved them as you have loved me" (John 17:23).

When believers are divided among themselves, their witness to the gospel is ineffectual. But, when believers live in harmony with one another, their lives become a declaration of God's name to the world that has a powerful effect. Why? Because strife hinders evangelism, but unity promotes evangelism.

Strife hinders evangelism. We can certainly see this in the scandals among a few noted televangelists in recent years. I can recall several conversations in which people have asked about my vocation. As soon as I tell them that I am a minister, they want to know my opinion concerning so-called fallen television evangelists. I have often wondered why the subject of Christianity or Christian ministry readily brings to mind names of prominent televangelists who have fallen into moral lapses rather than the name of Jesus Christ. Obviously, the rivalry and moral failures of those who would follow Christ diverts attention away from Christ. Jay Adams explains this tendency in these words:

> Whenever Christians squabble, the world cheers. That is because those whose hearts are turned against God, whose whole lives are one longstanding rivalry with Him, want to find any reason not to believe in Him. They do not want to surrender in repentance and faith or lay down their vendetta against God. Scandels among televangelists in which one accuses another of various indiscretions make front page copy in the media for weeks.(9)

When Christians are divided, we cannot hope to successfully win the world to Christ. Our lives speak louder than our words. In the eyes of the world, a divided church promotes an ineffectual gospel. Such a church does not hallow God's name by declaring it to the world. It does not enable the world to come to a knowledge of God.

As strife hinders evangelism, unity promotes evangelism. Jesus told His disciples that believers are to be the light of the world. Then He gave them this command: "Let your light shine before men, that they may see your good deeds and praise your Father in heaven" (Matthew 5:16). Now this puts a great deal of responsibility on the shoulders of believers. Only as others see the light of God's glory in the love and purity of our lives will they be able to acknowledge God's grace and give Him praise. It is our responsibility to live in unity with other believers so that our lives will reflect God to others. As the Apostle John said, "No one has ever seen God; but if we love one another, God lives in us and his love is made complete in us" (1 John 4:12). In reflecting God's grace through our love for one another, we hallow God's name before the world that others may come to know Him.

Summing It Up

In teaching us to address God as our heavenly Father and to hallow His name in prayer, Jesus has given us a prayer key that enables us to know God, worship God and reach the world for God. As we hallow God's name through acknowledging it, we come to know God. We know Him as our heavenly Father, our Lord and our Savior. As we hallow God's name through sanctifying it, we come to worship God. We worship Him as we open our hearts to Him to revere and adore Him. As we hallow God's name through declaring it, we come to reach the world for God. For through hallowing God's name as the Lord who saves, we are redeemed from sin and become one with the people of God. Our unity with fellow believers is the key to the evangelization of the world.

In the opening address and the first petition of the Lord's Prayer, Jesus has given us the key to our fellowship with God and our ministry in the world. Let's use this key often for the glory of God and the furtherance of His kingdom.

Notes

1. Douglas F. Kelly with Caroline S. Kelly, *If God Already Knows, Why Pray?* (Brentwood, Tennessee: Woglemuth & Hyatt, Publishers, Inc., 1989), p. 34.

2. From *The Gospel of Matthew*, (Volume 1: The Daily Study Bible Series) (Revised Edition), by William Barclay. Copyright © 1975 William Barclay. Used by permission of Westminster/John Knox Press and Saint Andrew Press, p. 203.

3. For a more comprehensive treatment of the names of God, see Larry Lea, *Could You Not Tarry One Hour* (Lake Mary, Florida: Creation House, 1987), pp. 55-78; Everett L. Fullam with Bob Slosser, *Living the Lord's Prayer* (Old Tappan, New Jersey: Fleming H. Revell Company, 1980), pp. 47-53; Rita Bennett, *Inner Wholeness Through The Lord's Prayer* (Tarrytown, New York: Fleming H. Revell Company, 1991), pp. 63-73; and Guy P. Duffield and N. M. Van Cleave, *Foundations of Pentecostal Theology* (Los Angeles: Life Bible College, 1983), pp. 62-68.

4. Smith Wigglesworth, *Ever Increasing Faith*, Revised edition (Springfield: Gospel Publishing House, 1971), pp. 28-33.

5. Robert Young, "Index-Lexicon To The New Testament," in *Young's Analytical Concordance to the Bible,*

Twenty-Second American Edition (Grand Rapids, Michigan: Wiliam B. Eerdmans Publishing Company, 1970), p. 72.

6. Everett L. Fullam with Bob Slosser, *Living The Lord's Prayer* (Old Tappan, New Jersey: Fleming H. Revell Company, 1980), pp.56-57.

7. John Wesley, *The Nature of the Kingdom*, Edited and updated by Clare George Weakley, Jr. (Minneapolis: Bethany House Publishers, 1979), p. 155.

8. Jay E. Adams, *Sibling Rivalry in the Household of God* (Denver, Colorado: Accent Books, 1988), p. 45.

Chapter Four

Prayer and The Kingdom

. . . your kingdom come, your will be done on earth as it is in heaven.—Matthew 6:10.

Madeleine L'Engle tells of an intriguing conversation she had with her children when they were small which was sparked by their questions concerning God's purposes in creation. The conversation proceeded as follows:

Why is there anything?
Well, God made something out of nothing.
Why? Didn't he like nothing?
Well, God is love, and it is the nature of love to create.
Could he have created anything he wanted to?
Of course. He's God.
Do you like what he created?
Yes. Yes, I do.
Battlefields and slums and insane asylums?

Well, he didn't create those.

Who did?

We did.

Who's we? I didn't create them.

Mankind did. And you're part of mankind and so am I.

But God created mankind?

Yes.

Why did he create mankind if mankind was going to create battlefields and slums and insane asylums?

I don't suppose that's what he created man *for*.

What did he create him for, then?

Well, it's the nature of love to create . . . (1)

L'Engle's attempt to respond to her children's questions concerning God's purposes in creation was, she admits, frustrating. Why? Because their questions were also her questions. Such frustrations are alleviated when the limits of reason bow in deference to the insights of revelation that come to us from the Bible.

The Scripture teaches that "God is love" (1 John 4:16). Furthermore, the Scripture supports the notion that God's love prompted Him to create. (See Ephesians 1:4-6.) But love is not blind. God, who sees the end from the beginning, knew that humankind would yield to temptation and fall into sin. He knew that sinful humanity would create battlefields and slums and insane asylums. But He also knew that His love would move Him to provide a way of redemption in sending His Son to be the Savior of the world. He knew that His Son would bring to the chaos of the fallen world the order and beauty of the kingdom of God for all who would receive it. And how are fallen men to receive God's kingdom? This question is answered in John's inspired words concerning the outcome of faith in Jesus: "Yet to all who received him, to those who believed in his name, he gave the right to become children of God—children born not of natural descent, nor of human decision or a husband's will, but born of God" (John 1:12,13).

The coming of the kingdom of God to earth in the person of Jesus and in the heart of every believer is the beginning of the end of the chaos and corruption of the fallen order. I say the beginning of the end because the kingdom of God has simply been introduced into the world through Christ and His Church. It will not come in its full manifestation of power and glory until God's judgments are poured out upon those who reject His kingdom reign and Christ returns to establish an unchallenged reign of justice and peace. Later we'll look at the biblical chart of events leading up to the full establishment of God's kingdom among humankind. It is sufficient here to note that the time in which we live is a time of transition in which we have already entered God's kingdom by faith in Christ and yet must continue to pray for the coming of God's kingdom in its full reality. In this transitional time between Christ's first coming and His final advent, the cry of our hearts must be expressed in the petition of the Lord's Prayer that concerns us in this chapter. Jesus taught us to pray, "Your kingdom come, your will be done on earth as it is in heaven" (Matthew 6:10).

The more fully we submit to God's reign in our own lives, the more effectively God will be able to use us toward the establishment of His kingdom in the earth. So then, to pray for the coming of God's kingdom is to pledge our personal submission to God the King. This chapter focuses upon our own responsibility to receive and submit to God's kingdom. To help us own God as our King, we're going to focus on the kingdom of God with a view to understanding what it is and how it affects our lives. We will talk about the kingdom of God as it relates to: our theology, our lives, our ministries and our prayers.

The Kingdom Of God In Our Theology

First of all, we must have a proper understanding of the kingdom of God before we can render a personal submission to God the King. Therefore, we will begin by focusing upon the kingdom of God in our theology. In our discussion, we will address three questions:

1. What is the kingdom of God?
2. How does it come?
3. What are its effects?

The first question that concerns us is a question of definition: What is the kingdom of God? The petition of the Lord's Prayer calling for the coming of God's kingdom actually answers this question for us. We are to pray, "Your kingdom come, your will be done on earth as it is in heaven." Now this verse is composed in the style of a particular kind of biblical poetic parallelism called synonymous parallelism. Accordingly, the first part of the verse and the second part of the verse say the same thing in different words. So then, to say, "Your kingdom come" means the same thing as saying, "Your will be done on earth as it is in heaven." How is God's will done in heaven? It is done willingly and joyfully. (See Psalm 103:20,21; Revelation 5:11,12.) In the light of this analysis, we can define the kingdom of God in the earth as God's reign upon the earth that elicits from the lives of human beings a willing and joyful obedience.

This is how Jesus defines the kingdom of God within the Lord's Prayer. To gain more precise understanding of what the kingdom of God is and how it comes to the earth, it will be helpful to see how the Jews of Jesus' day understood the kingdom of God and how Jesus' teaching on the subject compared with their understanding.

Among the Jews of Jesus' day, there were two conflicting views of the kingdom of God.(2) Some believed that the Messiah would come as a political figure who would crush the oppressors of God's people, the Jews, and would establish His sovereign rule in Israel. From His seat in Israel, the Messiah and the Jewish nation would rule the world. (See Daniel 7; Isaiah 9,11.) Other contemporaries of Christ were so psychologically overwhelmed by two centuries of persecution of the Jews that they despaired of associating the kingdom of God with Jewish nationalism. They believed that the present age was controlled by evil spirits that brought the vicious cycle of sin, sickness, disease and death into the earth. They looked for the coming of the Messiah as one anointed by God to destroy these evil spirits thus abolishing the present evil age. The Messiah would then introduce a new age in which He would rule the world in righteousness. (See Enoch 37-71.) This future reign of righteousness was to encompass the whole world and was to be the kingdom of God in the earth.

These two Jewish views of the kingdom of God were obviously conflicting. The first view looked for a Messiah who would bring a reign of righteousness through *political* force in the *present* age. The second view looked for a Messiah who would bring a reign of righteousness through *spiritual* force in a *future* age. Jesus' teaching about the kingdom of God embraced both these views but reversed their logic. First, the reign of righteousness would come through *spiritual* force in the *present* age. Jesus said, " . . . if I drive out demons by the finger of God, then the kingdom of God has come to you". (Luke 11:20) Second, the reign of righteousness would come in *political* form in a *future* age. Jesus said about the time of His second coming, "At that time the sign of the Son of Man will appear in the sky, and all the nations of the earth will mourn. They will see the Son of Man coming on the clouds of the sky with power and great glory" (Matthew 24:30). On that day, there will be loud voices in heaven saying, "The kingdom of the world has become the kingdom of our Lord and of his Christ, and he will reign for ever and ever" (Revelation 11:15).

To summarize, the kingdom of God in the earth is God's reign upon the earth that elicits from the lives of human beings a willing and joyful obedience. It comes in the present age insofar as spiritual forces of evil are dispelled and righteousness is effected in the hearts and lives of individuals who welcome God's reign over them. It will come in full force in a future age when Christ will return in power and glory to vanquish all evil from the earth and to establish an eternal reign of righteousness.

We have defined the kingdom of God as it relates to the life of human beings upon the earth. In doing so, we have spoken of the two *phases* in which God's kingdom comes to earth. It has come in the spiritual arena of life and will one day come in the political arena of this world. We turn now to the next question that concerns us: How does God's kingdom come? In answer, we will speak of three *vehicles* through which God's kingdom comes to the earth. God's kingdom comes to the earth through the vehicles of faith, ministry and prayer.

First of all, God's kingdom comes to the earth through faith. As we receive Jesus Christ as the Savior and Lord of our lives through faith, we become citizens of God's kingdom. Let's see just how this takes place.

God's kingdom came into the world in the person of Jesus Christ, Who perfectly submitted His own life to God's reign. God's kingdom comes to us through the person of Jesus Christ. Jesus bore our sins in His death and gave us His righteousness as our own. As Paul states, "God made him who had no sin to be sin for us, so that in him we might become the righteousness of God" (2 Corinthians 5:21). When we receive Jesus as the Savior and Lord of our lives by faith, our sins are forgiven and Christ's own righteousness is imparted to us as a gift. Christ's righteousness becomes our own. Thus God sees us as standing by faith in perfect submission to His reign. Through faith in Christ's redemptive work on our behalf, we have become citizens of God's kingdom. In this way God's kingdom comes to the earth through faith.

Second, God's kingdom comes to the earth through ministry. While the kingdom of God came into the world in the person of Jesus Christ, it comes into *manifestation* in the world only when its presence is proclaimed and its power is demonstrated. Such proclamation of the presence of God's kingdom and demonstration of the power of God's kingdom takes place through Christian ministry.

Jesus both proclaimed the presence and demonstrated the power of the kingdom. His ministry is described in part as " . . . preaching the good news of the kingdom and healing every disease and sickness" (Matthew 9:35). Jesus' disciples both proclaimed the presence and demonstrated the power of the kingdom. Jesus sent them out to minister with this command: "As you go, preach this message: 'The kingdom of heaven is near.' Heal the sick, raise the dead, cleanse those who have leprosy, drive out demons. Freely you have received, freely give" (Matthew 10:7,8.) Jesus' disciples in all ages are to both proclaim the presence and demonstrate the power of the kingdom. The Great Commission in Mark states: "Go into all the world and preach the good news to all creation. . . . And these signs will accompany those who believe: In my name they will drive out demons; . . . they will place their hands on sick people and they will get well" (Mark 16:15-18). We see that for Jesus, His immediate circle of disciples and His disciples *in all ages*, God's kingdom comes into manifestation where its presence is proclaimed through preaching and its power is demonstrated through healing the sick and driving out demons. By such proclamation and demonstration God's kingdom comes to the earth through the vehicle of ministry.

Third, the kingdom of God comes to earth through prayer. While the kingdom of God is initially received through faith in Christ's redemptive work and is shared with others through a ministry of proclamation and demonstration, the reign of God will come to the earth in its fullness only through the patient and persistent prayers of the saints. The saints are those who "have longed for

[Christ's] appearing" (2 Timothy 4:8) and whose constant prayer is "Come, Lord Jesus" (Revelation 22:20). In answer to the prayers of the saints, Christ will come again. His coming will trigger a series of events that will bring the kingdom of God in its fullness to earth. Let's see just how this will happen.

When Christ returns, the Christian dead will be raised and Satan will be bound and confined to the abyss for one thousand years. (See Revelation 20:1-3.) During that time, Christ and the saints will rule the earth, establishing a reign of righteousness (vs. 4). Isaiah describes this millennial reign of Christ and the saints as a time when all the peoples of the world will live peaceably with each other, and even wild animals will be as peaceful and playful as domesticated ones. (See Isaiah 2:4;11:6.) At the end of the millennial reign of Christ and the saints, Satan will be loosed from his confinement and will attempt yet again to deceive the people of the earth. (See Revelation 20:8.) He will gather the nations of the world in one large military array against the city of Jerusalem from which Christ is ruling the earth. When he does, fire will fall from heaven and consume the enemies of Israel (vs. 9). Then Satan will be cast into the fires of hell (vs. 10), and the unbelieving dead will be raised, judged and condemned (vs. 11-15). At that time, the heavenly city, the new Jerusalem, will descend as the saints of God from every nation enter into their inheritance (vs. 1-3). All sin, sorrow, sickness, pain, and death will be forever vanquished from God's people (vs. 4). This will mark the full manifestation of God's reign over the earth. It will come in answer to the patient and persistent prayers of the saints for the return of Christ.

Thus the kingdom of God will ultimately come to the earth in its fullness through the vehicle of prayer.

We've seen that the kingdom of God in the earth is God's reign upon the earth that elicits from the lives of human beings a willing and joyful obedience to God the King. This reign of righteousness and peace initially penetrates the spiritual dimension of life but ultimately dominates the political arena of the world. It is the reign of God over His people that comes to earth through the vehicles of faith in Christ's redemptive work, ministry that proclaims the presence and demonstrates the power of God's kingdom and prayer that hastens the return of Christ to establish God's rule over all the earth.

We now know what the kingdom of God is and how it comes. But what are its effects? This question is best answered in the words of the Apostle John, who wrote "The reason the Son of God appeared was to destroy the devil's work" (1 John 3:8). Jesus said, "The thief comes only to steal and kill and destroy; I have come that they may have life, and have it to the full" (John 10:10). These verses suggest the effects of the coming of God's kingdom to earth both in terms of the destruction of Satan's work and the establishment of God's work.

The effects of the coming of God's kingdom to the earth are, first of all, the destruction of Satan's work. A study of the ministry of Jesus and His disciples in the gospels and Acts makes it evident that the presence of the kingdom of God destroys the devil's works by delivering human beings from depravity, disease, demons and death. God's kingdom purpose is to deliver us not only from sin but from all of the effects of sin. This is what we are praying for when we petition God for the coming of His kingdom.

Second, the effects of the coming of God's kingdom to the earth are the establishment of God's work. For the presence of God's kingdom not only delivers believers *out of* the tyranny of Satan's rule. It also delivers them *into* the liberty of God's rule. We learn from the Apostle Paul that God's kingdom consists of "righteousness, peace and joy in the Holy Spirit" (Romans 14:17). For where God's kingdom is present and received, lives are transformed by God's grace with the effect that they are characterized by righteousness, peace and joy. On a social level, the result of such transformed lives will be that people will live together in justice, peace and love. This also is what we are praying for when we petition God for the coming of his kingdom.

As we have learned what the kingdom of God is, how it comes, and how it affects us, we have endeavored to lay a firm foundation for understanding God's kingdom. In doing so, we have focused upon the kingdom of God in our theology. We turn now to consider the kingdom of God in our lives.

The Kingdom Of God In Our Lives

We must have a proper biblical understanding of the kingdom of God. However, our understanding of God's kingdom is of no practical value to us unless we experience God's kingdom in our lives. And how do we experience God's kingdom in our lives? We do so through the surrender of our lives to God and the submission of our wills to God.

First, we must surrender our lives to God if we are to experience His kingdom. If we insist on running our own lives as we think best, then we reject the sovereign reign of God over us and opt to exercise sovereign rulership over ourselves. This is the essence of sin. But if we repent of the sin of rejecting God and in faith embrace His sovereign lordship over us, we can die to our rival kingdom of self and be born again as citizens of God's kingdom. Jesus taught that through faith in His redemptive work on our behalf we are born again enabling us to both see and enter God's kingdom. (See John 3:3,5,14.)

Second, we must submit our wills to God if we are to experience His kingdom. We must personalize the Lord's prayer as we pray, "Your kingdom come, your will be done *in my life* as it is in heaven." We must commit ourselves to prayerfully searching out God's will for our lives and obeying His every command and prompting.

If we are truly willing to do God's will, then He will make His will known to us. I learned this lesson the hard way in finding the right seminary for my graduate training. During my last semester in college, the time came for me to begin filing applications for graduate studies. A professor in the department of religion at my college advised me to apply to a divinity school that was a part of a large, well-respected university on the east coast of the United States. I applied, was accepted, and began my graduate work there the next fall. Before I had completed half of the first semester of studies, I was convinced that I had chosen the wrong school.

My first semester at the divinity school had me happily busy with four classes and a part-time job. But the challenge and the joy of graduate studies began to wane as my eyes became opened to the monster of theological liberalism. In three of my four classes (New Testament Greek excepted), the subject of the supernatural aspects of Christian ministry would come up from time to time. In every case, the professors treated the subject as a mythological aspect of an ancient worldview that is no longer tenable in the scientific age in which we live. Their perspective left no room for miracles, divine healing, or deliverance in an enlightened understanding of Christian ministry.

I found myself upon the horns of a dilemma. I knew God had called me to full-time Christian ministry. I knew the New Testament shows that ministry consists of both proclaiming and demonstrating the presence of God's kingdom — proclaiming it through preaching and teaching and demonstrating it through healing the sick and driving out demons. I knew that every aspect of Christian ministry that was relevant in the first century is relevant today. I have experienced in my own life salvation, deliverance from a classic case of demonization, and miraculous healing from migraine headaches and an undiagnosed chronic abdominal affliction. Yet I was attending a divinity school in which the very professors who were supposed to be training me for Christian ministry did not themselves believe in the biblical model and commission for such ministry. How could they train me for a ministry in which they themselves did not believe?

Kneeling by my bed, I presented the matter to the Lord. I prayerfully informed God that I had made a mistake in not seeking His will concerning my choice of schools for graduate studies. I informed Him that the evidence was abundantly clear that He was not pleased in my choice of schools, as the professors did not believe what his Word taught about Christian ministry. They were those "having a form of godliness, but denying the power thereof" (2 Timothy 3:5; KJV). I asked God to forgive me for not consulting Him as I should have in this important decision. Knowing that it was not God's will for me to stay with the divinity school, I asked the Lord to lead me to a place where the academics would be just as rigorous but whose professors would not deny the power of God. They must affirm and teach the supernatural aspects of Christian ministry. Then I asked, "God, when I leave here, where do you want me to go?" Immediately, the Lord spoke into my spirit the word "Fuller."

I had heard of the name "Fuller" but had no idea what kind of school it was or even where it was. So I went to the library and referenced a catalog of theological schools and seminaries in the United States and Canada. Sure enough, there was a Fuller Theological Seminary—2,500 miles away in Pasadena, California!

I wrote a letter to the Dean of Academic affairs of the divinity school I was attending, to make my withdrawal from the school official. In the letter, I mentioned the three professors by name who had spurned the supernatural aspect of our Lord's commission and stated specifically the things they had said that convinced me that their training was working at cross purposes with my calling. Without my permission, the Dean made three copies of the letter and gave one to each of the professors I had named.

A couple of days later, I was dining with a friend who understood and accepted my reasons for leaving the divinity school. He said to me, "Mark, have you thought about what school you'll attend when you leave here? It's not like you to just give up and quit." Up to that point, I had not breathed a word to anyone about Fuller. Knowing that God had already spoken to me about it, however, I smiled and said, "I'm thinking about Fuller." As soon as I said this, my friend looked at me startled and blurted out "Fuller!" I said, somewhat sheepishly, "Yeah, what's wrong with Fuller?" He replied, "Oh, nothing. It's just that, well, our church history professor stopped me on the sidewalk today and said, `Gee, I'm sorry that your friend, Mark, is leaving us. Where is he planning to go, anyway? Fuller?'"

Amazing confirmation! Apparently, my church history professor at the divinity school knew of Fuller's reputation. When he read his copy of my letter of withdrawal and saw my reasons for leaving the divinity school, he figured the most likely school that I would choose would be Fuller.

I did not know it at the time, but Fuller Theological Seminary was receiving national recognition as a multi-denominational evangelical seminary that was teaching a pioneer course on the subject of supernatural signs and wonders both from a biblical perspective and with contemporary application.(3) The course was called MC510: "Signs, Wonders, and Church Growth." It was jointly introduced into the curriculum by professor of church growth Dr. C. Peter Wagner and adjunct professor John Wimber and was predominantly taught by professor Wimber. The course was attracting the largest enrollment of any class in the seminary. Furthermore, miraculous signs and wonders were taking place during the personal ministry time right in the classroom.

God's direction was clear, and I was determined to obey. I am now an alumnus of Fuller Theological Seminary and endeavoring to pursue God's call upon my life in full-time Christian ministry through the proclamation of the presence and the demonstration of the power of God's kingdom.

I learned through this experience that when we are truly willing to do God's will, He will make His will known to us. But we must prayerfully seek out His will for us and then submit our wills to Him in obedience. We should do this every time we personalize the Lord's prayer with the petition, "Your kingdom come, your will be done *in my life* as it is in heaven." The result will be that we will both enter into and experience the kingdom of God in our lives.

The Kingdom Of God In Our Ministries

Once we've come to understand the kingdom of God biblically and to experience it personally, we are ready to see it transform our ministries. To suggest how this takes place, we turn now to consider the kingdom of God in our ministries. In doing so, we will endeavor to point out just how we are to make the kingdom of God the centerpiece of our ministries in fulfilling both Jesus' evangelistic mandate and His social mandate.

We must first make the kingdom of God the centerpiece of our ministries by fulfilling Jesus' evangelistic mandate, or His commission to us to proclaim the gospel to every creature. And what is the gospel? It is the good news that Jesus—in his death, burial and resurrection—has effectively brought God's kingdom to earth and abolished Satan's reign. It is the good news that those who put their faith in Jesus immediately become subjects of God's kingdom and are delivered from the tyranny of Satan's domain.

How are we to fulfill the evangelistic mandate in our ministries? We must follow the biblical model and commission. We've already seen that Jesus and His disciples proclaimed the presence of God's kingdom through preaching and teaching and demonstrated its power through healing the sick and driving out demons. We've also seen from Mark's account of the Great Commission that such proclamation of the presence and demonstration of the power of God's kingdom should characterize the ministry of all believers in all ages. Every one of us is responsible to share the gospel, heal the sick, and drive out demons in our individual spheres of influence. In doing so, we make the kingdom of God the centerpiece of our ministries in fulfilling the evangelistic mandate.

Western Christians today often interpret the evangelistic mandate of our Lord in the light of advancements of science and technology. In doing so, they draw three conclusions. First, preaching the gospel, i.e. proclaiming the presence of the kingdom, is the Christian responsibility of the clergy. Secondly, driving out evil spirits is a primitive way of treating the mentally and emotionally ill. Treating such illness today is the Christian responsibility of mental health professionals. Thirdly, healing the sick is the Christian responsibility of medical doctors.

In all due respect to Western Christians, mental health specialists and medical practitioners, such compartmentalization of the tasks involved in fulfilling the evangelistic mandate of our Lord's Great Commission is foreign to the Scriptures. For the evangelistic mandate contained in the

Great Commission was not given to specialists in theology, psychology and medicine. It was given to *all* Christians in all ages. In this mandate and commission, Jesus clearly commanded that all believers are to preach the gospel of the kingdom, drive out evil spirits (not mental illnesses) and heal the sick. (See Mark 16:15-18.)

The manner in which proper emphasis upon the kingdom of God fulfills the evangelistic mandate is helpfully illustrated by the formative stages of the phenomenal ministry of John Wimber, pastor of the Vineyard Christian Fellowship of Anaheim, California.(4) For a dozen years as a Christian, Wimber had been taught that the kingdom of God has no significant bearing upon Christian life and ministry in the present as God's kingdom will not come to the earth until Jesus returns. But Wimber's views began to change in 1974 when he joined the staff of Fuller Theological Seminary's Department of Church Growth. Through the writings of the late George Eldon Ladd, a former professor in the School of Theology at Fuller, Wimber was led to reread and reconsider the teaching of the gospels concerning God's kingdom. He states the results of his study in these words: "I realized that at the very heart of the gospel lies the kingdom of God, and that power for effective evangelism and discipleship relates directly to our understanding and experiencing the kingdom today."

As Wimber realized a direct relationship in Scripture between the presence of God's kingdom and the manifestation of healing miracles, he began to pray for the sick in his church in 1977 with minimal effect. He saw a noticeable breakthrough in the ministry of healing in 1981. It was then that his friend David Watson invited him to teach on the subject of the kingdom of God in England.

Wimber's first meetings in England were with the parish of Bishop David Pytches' —St. Andrew's Anglican Church in Chorleywood, Hertfordshire. The first evening, Wimber spoke on healing and prayed for the sick with the minimal results he was used to. But the next morning the breakthrough came. Even though some in this "proper Anglican" parish were disturbed by the emphasis on healing, Wimber received Pytches' permission to proceed again in praying for the sick. As he did, a woman who was blind in one eye and another who was confined to a wheelchair with multiple sclerosis were both completely healed. What was the result? That evening one hundred young people gave their lives to God. Many of them have since become ministers.

From Chorleywood, Wimber went to York to minister in the parish of his friend David Watson—St. Michael-le-Belfrey. Again the results were quite supernatural with people being healed, delivered from demons and saved.

At the close of Wimber's ministry time in England, David Watson and a colleague escorted him to the train station when the colleague asked Watson, "Well, how are you going to describe this week to the bishop?" He was referring to a written report that Watson was required to submit to the bishop concerning special meetings at his parish. Watson replied, "I don't think it will be difficult to write about what happened. I'll report, `The blind receive sight, the lame walk . . . and the good news is preached to the poor.'" These words are, in part, a quotation from Matthew 11:5 through which Jesus sought to confirm his Messiahship to the doubtful John the Baptist. For Wimber, it was confirmation that he had faithfully made the kingdom of God the centerpiece of his ministry in so proclaiming the kingdom and demonstrating its power as to effectively fulfill Jesus' evangelistic mandate.

If we are to make God's kingdom the centerpiece of our ministries by fulfilling the evangelistic mandate, we too must embrace Jesus' commission in its totality and not simply those parts of His commission that are fashionable to the contemporary world. Our ministries are not going to be effective in accomplishing God's purposes unless they are characterized by the proclamation of the presence and the demonstration of the power of God's kingdom. Our responsibility is to witness concerning the presence of God's reign among humankind and to pray for the healing of the sick and the deliverance of the demonized. As we prove faithful in our part, God will take responsibility to bring the results.

We make God's kingdom the centerpiece of our ministries not only through fulfilling Jesus' evangelistic mandate, but also through fulfilling His social mandate. Now by the social mandate, I mean Jesus' commission to us to care for the needs of the poor and the oppressed. Without such concern, the gospel cannot be fully proclaimed nor fully demonstrated.

We must understand that preaching the gospel, healing the sick, and driving out demons does not assure that we have done the whole will of God. Jesus warned concerning the day of judgment, "Many will say to me on that day, 'Lord, Lord, did we not prophesy in your name, and in your name drive out demons and perform many miracles?' Then I will tell them plainly, 'I never knew you. Away from me, you evildoers!' (Matthew 7:22,23). Jesus had something else interesting to say about the day of judgment. On that day, Jesus will separate the sheep from the goats, i.e. the righteous from the unrighteous. Then he will welcome the righteous to enter into their inheritance—the kingdom of God in its ultimate form. And on what grounds does He welcome them? Here is the answer in Jesus' own words:

> For I was hungry and you gave me something to eat, I was thirsty and you gave me something to drink, I was a stranger and you invited me in, I needed clothes and you clothed me, I was sick and you looked after me, I was in prison and you came to visit me . . . I tell you the truth, whatever you did for one of the least of these brothers of mine, you did for me—Matthew 25:35,36,40.

The balance of these two passages suggests that if one is truly saved by grace through faith, the fruit of his salvation will be both the fulfillment of the evangelistic mandate and the social mandate. That is, he will not only preach the gospel, heal the sick, and drive out demons but will also care for the needs of the hungry, the lonely, the sickly, and the incarcerated—in short, all those who are suffering. Thus he will make the kingdom of God the centerpiece of his ministry through fulfilling not just the evangelistic mandate but the social mandate as well.

The tendency to fulfill the evangelistic mandate and to neglect the social mandate must be avoided at all costs. Yet it is all too easy to develop this tendency unless we walk in genuine humility and love. Evangelist Arthur Blessitt pointed out that many Christians will visit a person who is sick and pray for his healing. If the person does not get healed, however, they will criticize him for being either in need of repentance for some undisclosed sin or deficient in faith. Having laid this guilt trip on the sick individual, they will not go back again to minister Christian love by comforting him in his affliction and encouraging him in his time of distress. This certainly does not reflect the patience and love of God for His children.

As we ponder this example of hard-heartedness toward the suffering, we come to realize that humility and patience are essential if we are to effectively minister to the suffering and dejected. There are many who are crying inside because they feel inadequate to deal with the pressures of life that have adversely affected their emotional and physical health. It may very well be the case that their plight is due to neglecting spiritual disciplines in their lives and that repentance and faith are essential keys to their recovery. However, in order to learn the lessons that will put them on the road to their recovery, they need the fellowship of caring Christians who are humble enough to stick with them through their frustrations and patient enough to guide them toward progress in wholeness and Christian growth. It is as we exemplify such love expressed in humility and patience that we will be able to fulfill the social mandate in caring for the suffering and dejected.

The social mandate not only requires loving ministry to the suffering and dejected, but also requires such ministry to those who are poor and needy. Many Christians who are ready to come to the aid of those who are suffering and dejected have little patience with the poor and needy. If we are to make the kingdom of God the centerpiece of our ministries through the fulfillment of the social mandate, however, we must give high priority to providing for the poor.

God taught me an important lesson about ministry to the poor. During my seminary years, I saw how the poor and homeless live. While Los Angeles is known for its street people, Pasadena—just 20 miles south of L.A. — has its share of them as well. As a student with living expenses, high tuition costs and a moderate income from a part-time job, I felt frustrated at times in meeting such needy people and having few resources with which to help them. Often, to conserve gas, I walked several blocks to work or to school. Almost every time, street people stopped me and asked for help. Sometimes, I helped them with a dollar or two.

It wasn't long before I grew suspicious of street people. I noticed that they all asked for "a little loose change" for food or said that their car was "stranded on the freeway" and they needed gas. These seemed to be pet phrases with them. I wondered if maybe they were con-artists who met and talked about what tactics worked the best in playing upon people's sympathies and getting money out of them. My suspicions seemed to be confirmed when the seminary student newsletter, "The Semi," came out with a short article warning students against street people who loved to prey upon the caring Christians at the seminary who were "easy pickin's." Nonetheless, my heart told me that some of the street people were not hucksters but had legitimate needs that God would not have us ignore. The question in my mind was how to tell the real from the phony.

On one occasion, I was invited by a friend out to dinner. After we left the restaurant, a man approached me with an empty gas can. He informed me that his car was "stranded on the freeway" and asked if I would give him a couple of bucks for gas. I decided not to give him money but to offer to walk with him to the service station across the street and put a couple of dollars worth of gas in the can for him.

As we crossed the street, a Volkswagen bug driven by another seminary student slowed down and stopped on the highway. From the passenger's window, a man extended his arm with gas can in hand and yelled out, "That's okay, man, we've already got some gas!" I looked at him and asked, "Just where is your car anyway?" He pointed in the opposite direction of the freeway!

Disgusted, I turned to walk away. The man who had originally stopped me asked, "Hey, aren't you going to help us?" I replied, "You've already got your gas." He said, "But we need more gas than that to get to where we're going." I asked, "But why did you lie to me? You told me your car was stranded on the freeway and your partner pointed away from the freeway!" He said, "I guess he got it started and pulled it off the freeway." Not wanting to judge him but give him the benefit of the doubt, I went ahead and gave him a couple of dollars to get some more gas.

God later used this story to teach me a valuable lesson about caring for the poor. An assignment for a Christian ethics class drove the lesson home. I had to write a "moral dilemma" paper describing a hypothetical situation concerning a human need that required wisdom in responding appropriately in a Christian manner. Using scriptural principles pertaining to Christian ethics, I had to decide upon the genuinely Christian response. I used the incident that I just related as my hypothetical situation. My conclusion was based upon the following points: First, Jesus said, "Give to everyone who asks you, and if anyone takes what belongs to you, do not demand it back" (Luke 6:30). Second, this statement is made in a context that calls for a willing vulnerability to those who might try to take advantage of your goodness. Third, the writer of Hebrews states, "Do not forget to entertain strangers, for by so doing some people have entertained angels without knowing it" (13:2). The ethical principles contained in these insights from Scripture led me to the conclusion that the genuinely Christian response would be to give the man the money for gas that he requested even if he might actually be a huckster in disguise as a stranded traveler.

As I pulled the last page of this paper from my typewriter, I laughed and said out loud, "That sounds right, but I probably wouldn't do it." After putting my typewriter away, I started to fix dinner. Because it was a holiday, I changed my mind and decided to go out and eat. I drove a couple of blocks to a nearby restaurant. I had parked my car and was walking to the restaurant when for the first time in months a man approached me with a gas can! Would I help him buy some gas for his stranded car? How could I say no when just five minutes earlier I had persuasively argued that the genuinely Christian response would be to take the stranger at his word and offer the help desired? Not wanting to be a hypocrite, I welcomed this stranger as though he were an angel of God and treated him and his sister to some food and some gas for his "stranded" car.

My experience communicates an important lesson. If we are to minister to those who are poor and needy, we must guard ourselves against the tendency to be suspicious of the motives or truthfulness of those who appeal to us for help. We must be willing to make ourselves vulnerable to those who just might take advantage of our goodness. Otherwise, we may turn away those with genuine needs and thus fail to communicate the love of God to the poor. If we are worried about not having sufficient means to help them and take care of our own obligations, we need to be reminded of a promise and a warning from Scripture. The promise of Scripture is this: "He who is kind to the poor lends to the Lord, and he will reward him for what he has done" (Proverbs 19:17). The warning of Scripture is this: "If a man shuts his ears to the cry of the poor, he too will cry out and not be answered" (Proverbs 21:13). We must be kind to the poor if we are to fulfill Jesus' social mandate and so make the kingdom of God the centerpiece of our ministries.

The Kingdom Of God In Our Prayers

The greatest aid to our understanding God's kingdom, our experiencing its presence in our lives, and our imparting its blessings to others through our ministries is to be found in praying consistently and in faith, "Your kingdom come, your will be done in earth as it is in heaven." For this reason, we conclude this chapter by considering the kingdom of God in our prayers. In this connection, we'll say a word about how praying for the coming of God's kingdom affects our prayers both in terms of method and of content.

Praying for the coming of God's kingdom the way Jesus taught us affects the method of our praying. It causes us to pray forcefully. This is communicated in the grammatical structure of the petition of the Lord's Prayer with which we are presently concerned. In the Greek, the verbs in this verse are placed at the beginning of their respective clauses. Larry Lea suggests how this grammatical arrangement affects the meaning of the verse when he renders the first part of the verse to read, "Come, kingdom of God! Be done, will of God!"(5) Lea depicts the import of the verse as being like a man who decisively puts his foot down and declares how things will be done.

It is not unusual that Jesus would teach us to pray forcefully for the coming of God's kingdom. It agrees with His teaching about the kingdom of God elsewhere. For instance, Jesus said, "From the days of John the Baptist until now, the kingdom of heaven has been forcefully advancing, and forceful men lay hold of it" (Matthew 11:12). God would have us to boldly venture forth and take the kingdom as it advances toward us.

I learned this lesson in a very memorable way in the winter of 1988. I was doing a seminary internship at the time for the Trinity Assembly of God Church of Pasadena, California. One day, I received a call from an acquaintance by the name of Greg Ryan who worked in middle management for the Pacific Bell Telephone Company of Studio City, California. Greg and I had met about a year earlier at a small park in Pasadena where I had opportunity to offer healing prayer for a prostate condition that he had contracted nineteen years earlier. At the time of that prayer, the symptoms of infection had been constant for ten months. Within a day of prayer, he was considerably better. Within three days, he was totally healed. Now Greg was calling for one of his employees—Anne Jones. She had a short leg and wore a built-up shoe. Greg asked if I would be willing to meet with and pray for her. I assured him that I would. We contacted Anne and made an appointment.

On the day of the appointment, I met Anne at the church where I was interning. She immediately recognized the place. She informed me that she used to attend church there. She also admitted that she had backslidden in her walk with God. I knew that her greatest need was to be restored to fellowship with the Lord.

When I inquired about her condition, I learned that her physical condition was much more extensive than I had been told. She had fallen in her home in 1981—seven years earlier—and fractured three vertebrae in her lower back. In the interest of alleviating the severe pain, she had submitted to reconstructive surgery at the risk of possible extensive paralysis. After surgery, the pain was considerably less. She now described it as comparable to a constant toothache in her back which kept her from being able to sit flat on a seat. She had to shift from side to side when sitting. As for paralysis, the surgery had left her extremely numb from the left hip to the knee and totally paralyzed from the knee to the bottom of the foot. She could walk but could not go up and down steps without a walker.

I shared with Anne from the Scripture for several minutes before praying for her. I pointed out to her that Jesus, in His death, had purchased a complete salvation for her which included the forgiveness of her sins and the healing of her body. We looked together at Isaiah 53:5: "But he was pierced for our transgressions, he was crushed for our iniquities; the punishment that brought us peace was upon him, and by his wounds we are healed." I pointed out that her restored fellowship with God was more important than her physical healing and was, in fact, a key to keeping her physical healing. We looked together at John 5:14: "See, you are well again. Stop sinning or something worse may happen to you." And then I said something to her that I do not ordinarily say to people for whom I pray. Yet the words just seemed to escape my lips before I had a chance to ponder them. I said, "When I pray for you, God will heal you! But unless you rededicate your life to the Lord and live for Him, you will be in danger of losing your healing."

Let me point out the significance of that statement. Under the unction of the Holy Spirit, I declared, "When I pray for you, God will heal you!" In effect, that statement affirmed. "I take the kingdom by force! I put my foot down and declare how it is going to be!" Now some would call that presumption. And perhaps it would have been presumption if God had not moved me to say it before I could think about it. Under the unction of the Holy Spirit, however, I was doing exactly what Jesus taught us to do in the Lord's Prayer. I was saying, in effect, "Come, kingdom of God! Be done, will of God!" The Bible shows that it is God's will to reclaim the hearts of backsliders and to heal the sick.

Getting back to the story, I led Anne in a prayer of rededication as she renewed her fellowship with the Lord. Then, I had her sit as level as she could and extend her legs straight out in front of her. Even with wearing the built-up shoe, Anne's left leg was still shorter than the right by about half an inch. In accordance with Mark 11:23 in which Jesus taught us about the direct command of faith, I spoke to the left leg and commanded it in Jesus' name to grow out to full length. It instantly grew out in my hand. This kind of healing was not new to me—but the rest was. Within thirty seconds or so, all the paralysis left her leg and the pain entirely left her back! She was able to sit flat with no pain. Then she walked up and down the steps from the altar to the pulpit without her walker. This was the first time in seven years that she could walk up and down steps without a walker. Praise God!

When we pray for the coming of God's kingdom, we are to pray forcefully as we become the spiritually violent who take the blessings of God's kingdom by force. I have illustrated how this works in praying for the specific kingdom blessing of physical healing. The same principle applies in petitioning heaven for any kingdom blessing. Whether we are praying for deliverance from a sinful habit, freedom from mental and emotional distress, healing from sickness and disease, provision for a financial need or any other blessing by which God would lead his people into the abundant life, we are to pray forcefully as those who gratefully receive from the benevolent hand of God and violently rend from the obstructing clutches of the devil that which God has provided for us through the redemptive work of Christ on our behalf.

We've seen that praying for the coming of God's kingdom as Jesus taught us to affects the method of our prayers. We will pray forcefully. Thus we will be used of God in aggressively establishing the kingdom of God in the earth. Let me add that praying for the coming of God's kingdom as Jesus taught us to also affects the content of our prayers. Our prayers will appropriate the *present* blessings of the kingdom and appeal for the *future* blessings of the kingdom.

In praying for the coming of God's kingdom, our prayers appropriate the *present* blessings of the kingdom. They are saying in essence, "God, Your kingdom has already come into the earth for all of those who will receive it by faith. Now I pray in faith that it will come to my life that I may enjoy and share its blessings." How does this approach to praying for the coming of the kingdom affect the content of our prayers? Our prayers decree God's answers into every problematic situation of life. For our weakness, we decree God's strength. For our sickness, we decree God's healing. For our lack, we decree God's provision. Through prayer, we take the kingdom by force with full assurance of the verity of Jesus' words. "Do not be afraid, little flock, for your Father has been pleased to give you the kingdom" (Luke 12:32).

In praying for the coming of God's kingdom, our prayers not only appropriate the *present* blessings of the kingdom. They also appeal for the *future* blessings of the kingdom. For all that we have said about the presence and power of God's kingdom in the earth, some still fail to receive God's salvation, healing, deliverance, and blessing. The world still has its battlefields and slums and insane asylums. Satan is still "the god of this age" (2 Corinthians, 4:4) busily at work devising and utilizing his schemes of deception and destruction. As we pray for the coming of God's kingdom to earth, we are praying for the return of

Jesus who will execute Satan's final destruction and effect the world's grand liberation. We are praying for Jesus to establish an unchallenged reign of righteousness and peace among men. These are the future blessings of the kingdom for which we appeal when we pray for the coming of God's kingdom.

Summing It Up

God intends for our prayer lives to be the vehicle by which His kingdom comes to the earth. For that reason, the center of all our prayers should be in accord with the petition, "Your kingdom come, your will be done on earth as it is in heaven" (Matthew 6:10). In praying this petition, we pledge our personal submission to God our King and pledge our lives to His service. Such commitment is evidenced by the fact that we give the kingdom of God first priority in relation to our theology, our lives, our ministries and our prayers.

First, we give the kingdom of God first priority in relation to our theology. We have responded to three questions to help us along these lines. What is the kingdom of God? In relation to the human race it is defined as God's reign on the earth that elicits from the lives of human beings a willing and joyful obedience. How does it come? It comes to believers through personal faith in Jesus Christ. It comes to the world through the proclamation of its presence by way of preaching and teaching and through the demonstration of its power through healing the sick and driving out demons. It will come in its fullness through the patient and persistent prayers of the saints for the return of Christ, facilitating the final triumph of righteousness. What are its effects? It destroys the works of the devil which include sin and all of its effects—i.e. depravity, disease, demons and death. It also establishes the work of God which includes righteousness, peace and joy in the human heart and justice, peace and love in the human community.

Second, we give the kingdom of God first priority in relation to our lives. We come to experience God's kingdom in our lives when we surrender our lives and submit our wills to God. As we prayerfully seek out God's will for our lives with a sincere desire to perform it, God will make His will known to us. In doing God's will for our individual lives, we come to experience God's kingdom reign in us.

Third, we give the kingdom of God first priority in relation to our ministries. We have seen that we must make the kingdom of God the centerpiece of our ministries through fulfilling both the evangelistic mandate and the social mandate. We fulfill the evangelistic mandate through preaching the gospel, healing the sick, and driving out demons. We fulfill the social mandate through ministering in humility and patience to the suffering and dejected and through ministering in trust and a willing vulnerability to the poor and needy.

Finally, we give the kingdom of God first priority in relation to our prayers. We've pointed out that the greatest aid to understanding God's kingdom in our theology, experiencing God's kingdom in our lives and sharing God's kingdom through our ministries is in consistently and earnestly praying, "Your kingdom come, your will be done on earth as it is in heaven." As we pray this prayer, we are praying aggressively. We are putting our foot down and declaring that God's kingdom will be. We are appropriating the present blessings of God's kingdom as we decree God's blessing into every problematic situation of our lives. We are appealing for the future blessings of God's kingdom as we pray for Christ's return and the final triumph of righteousness.

It is appropriate that the final point of our discussion in this chapter has concerned us with the kingdom of God in our prayers. For it is in answer to our prayers for the coming of God's kingdom that we experience his kingdom in our lives and are enabled to pass on its blessings to others through our ministries. Furthermore, it is through our prayers for the coming of God's kingdom that we hasten the return of Christ to establish a reign of righteousness and peace on earth through which God's kingdom in its full-blown reality will come to the earth. So then, it is in the interest of bringing God's rule to bear in our lives, our ministries, and our world that we are to faithfully and joyfully pray with Jesus, "... your kingdom come, your will be done on earth as it is in heaven."

Notes

1. Madeleine L'Engle, *The Irrational Season* (New York: Harper Collins Publishers, 1977), p. 5.

2. George Eldon Ladd, *A Theology of the New Testament* (Grand Rapids, Michigan: William B. Eerdman's Publishing Company, 1974), p. 61.

3. See the special issue coverage: *Signs and Wonders Today*, Compiled by the Editors of Christian Life Magazine with the cooperation of C. Peter Wagner, Professor of Church Growth, Fuller Theological Seminary (Wheaton, Illinois: Christian Life Missions, 1983); and C. Peter Wagner, *How To Have A Healing Ministry Without Making Your Church Sick* (Ventura, California: Regal Books, 1988), pp. 47-50.

4. From *Kingdom Come*, Copyright ©1988 by John Wimber. Published by Servant Publications, Box 8617, Ann Arbor, Michigan 48107. Used with Permission, pp. 7-12.

5. Used by permission of Creation House, Lake Mary, Florida from *Could You Not Tarry One Hour?* by Larry Lea. Copyright ©1987, pp. 82,83.

PART THREE

The Circumference Of

The Lord's Prayer

Give us today our daily bread.
Forgive us our debts,
as we also have forgiven our debtors.
And lead us not into temptation,
but deliver us from the evil one,
for yours is the kingdom and the power
and the glory forever. Amen.
(Matthew 6:11-13)

Chapter Five

Kingdom Provision

Give us today our daily bread.—Matthew 6:11.

Biblical prosperity is a much debated topic among evangelical Christians. On one extreme are those who teach what is referred to by their critics as a "Health, Wealth and Prosperity Gospel." Their approach to prayer is generally dubbed "name it and claim it." Some advocates of this theology run the risk of becoming overly materialistic as they pursue lifestyles of luxury in the name of biblical prosperity. On the other extreme are those who teach that poverty is a virtue because it keeps one from becoming worldly. Their approach to prayer is one of passive resignation to God's sovereign will. In my estimation, some advocates of this theology run the risk of missing many of the blessings that God desires for them. Why? Because they shun God's promises to prosper them and do not pray with specific, persistent petitions for the fulfillment of those promises.

When it comes to the subject of biblical prosperity, dangers are to be avoided on both sides of the road. As with many subjects, a biblical balance is needed. Our text for this chapter provides that biblical balance, because it teaches us how to prosper on God's terms rather than our own.

God's formula for prosperity can be stated this way: As we give priority in our lives *to* God's kingdom, we will receive provision for our needs *through* God's kingdom. When we tend to God's business, God tends to our business. This truth should inspire us to find in our allegiance to God's kingdom the source of our personal prosperity and blessing.

This chapter focuses upon the petition of the Lord's Prayer that concerns our prosperity. Jesus taught us to pray, saying, "Give us today our daily bread" (Matthew 6:11). He encouraged us to appeal to God our King for the meeting of our daily needs. In order to pray this prayer in faith and confidence, we must rightly understand what the Bible teaches about our prosperity. For that reason, we will present our discussion under three headings:

1. God's purpose for our prosperity
2. God's preconditions for our prosperity
3. God's plan for our prosperity

God's Purpose For Our Prosperity

Let's begin by discussing God's purpose for our prosperity. Stated more precisely, it is our intention here to establish the point that it is God's purpose for us that we prosper. God wants us to have our needs met rather than being content to go without basic necessities and the things that are good for us.

While it should be evident that God wants His children to prosper, Christians often speak of poverty as though it were a virtue. Historically, religious orders have often required their postulants to take vows of poverty. The implication is that not having worldly riches makes it all the easier to prevent one's heart from becoming attached to this passing world. Thus the postulant is able to set his heart fully upon God and His kingdom. While the Bible warns that worldly wealth can steal our hearts away from God and His kingdom, (see Mark 10:24,25), the Bible also maintains that God desires to teach us to use the things of the world without becoming engrossed in them. (See 1 Corinthians 7:31.) This kind of detachment is an essential aspect of biblical prosperity.

We learn from the Lord's Prayer that God desires for us to prosper on His terms. And what are His terms? As we give priority in our lives to God's kingdom, we will receive provision for our needs through God's kingdom. Stated succinctly, kingdom priority produces kingdom provision. This is a principle that Jesus both taught and demonstrated.

Jesus taught the principle that kingdom priority produces kingdom provision. We can see this principle of biblical prosperity in the Lord's Prayer as we notice the arrangement of its petitions. We address God as our heavenly Father, we hallow His name in worship and adoration and we petition for the coming of His kingdom and the establishment of His will in the earth. Only then we pray, "Give us today our daily bread" (Matthew 6:11). We first acknowledge God as our king and submit to His kingly reign over us. Then we appeal to Him for His kingdom provision by which He meets our needs.

The fact that kingdom priority produces kingdom provision is not simply an incidental point that comes to the fore in the Lord's Prayer. It is a point that is characteristic of the teaching of the Sermon on the Mount as a whole. It is summarized in one of the most quoted verses of the Sermon on the Mount. Having instructed His disciples not to worry about the basic needs of life, Jesus stated: "But seek first [God's] kingdom and his righteousness, and all these things will be given to you as well" (Matthew 6:33). In short, as we give God's kingdom first place in our lives, we will be aptly provided for through the resources of His kingdom.

Jesus not only taught this principle of biblical prosperity. He demonstrated it. Let me give two examples from the gospels that illustrate the point.

Jesus demonstrated the principle that kingdom priority produces kingdom provision at His first encounter with Simon Peter. (See Luke 5:1-11.) Simon was fishing one day when Jesus befriended him and used his boat as a platform from which to preach to the crowd gathered along the shoreline. After ministering to the people, Jesus turned to Peter and said, "Put out into deep water, and let down the nets for a catch" (vs. 4). Peter replied, "Master, we've worked hard all night and haven't caught anything. But because you say so, I will let down the nets" (vs. 5).

This discouraged fisherman hadn't caught any fish. On this particular day, his labor had proven futile in providing for his family. Yet one gets the sense that he had deep respect for the rabbi, Jesus. He humbly submitted to Jesus' instruction. And what was the result? He instantly pulled in so many fish that it took his boat and the boat of two colleagues to pull the fish to shore.

When Peter saw the tremendous catch, he fell at Jesus' feet in humility and shame. He said, "Go away from me, Lord; I am a sinful man!" (vs. 9). But Jesus' response was assuring: "Don't be afraid; from now on you will catch men" (vs. 10).

What was Jesus communicating to Peter? Let me suggest an answer. Perhaps Peter was the kind of person who worked hard to support his family and would never dream of leaving his work without the assurance of financial security. Jesus saw in Peter a man called by God to be His disciple. Respecting Peter's concern for the sustenance of his family, Jesus performed this miracle to assure Peter that God sufficiently takes care of His own. Once Peter saw this to be the case, he was ready to join Jesus and go fishing for men. Jesus was teaching Peter, in effect, that if he would put God's kingdom interests ahead of his own concern for financial security, God would prove faithful in providing for all of his needs. Thus Peter was learning that kingdom priority produces kingdom provision.

Through another, equally remarkable miracle, Jesus demonstrated this principle of biblical prosperity to a crowd of 5,000 men plus women and children. (See Matthew 14:13-21.) Jesus spent a full day ministering to these people out of the resources of God's kingdom. Specifically, we read that, "He had compassion on them and healed their sick" (vs. 14). When the evening arrived, Jesus miraculously fed the entire crowd with five small loaves of bread and two fish. When everyone had his fill, twelve basketfuls of leftovers were collected (vs. 20). They ended up with more food than they started with! And what was the purpose of this miracle? To teach the crowd this principle: because they gave priority to God's kingdom that day, they experienced God's provision for their needs. They learned experientially that kingdom priority produces kingdom provision.

The principle holds true for us today. If we give priority in our lives to God's kingdom, our needs will be met through God's kingdom. God demonstrated this fact to me in a memorable way when I was in seminary.

When I first began seminary, I decided not to borrow any money to pay for my schooling. My conviction was based on God's clear counsel in the Bible. The writer of Proverbs says, "The rich rule over the poor, and the borrower is servant to the lender" (22:7). The Apostle Paul adds, "Owe no man anything, but to love one another" (Romans 13:8). I felt that God had called me to the ministry and had specified the seminary I was to attend by name. I was obeying Him and putting His kingdom first by being in school. Therefore, I would trust Him to provide any money I needed beyond support from my dad, from my part-time job and from the financial assistance that had been made available to me through an academic grant.

During one particular quarter, I needed $494.67 to pay the rest of my tuition for the current quarter before I would be permitted to register for the next quarter. A couple of weeks before registration, I was walking toward the campus post office with another student when she said, "I'm afraid I'm going to have to drop out of school." "You're not serious!" I replied. "You're not planning to quit school, are you?"

"Oh, no!" she said. "Only for one quarter. I don't have the money to finish paying my current tuition. I'm going to have to work full-time for a while to afford to stay in school."

Not meaning to sound proud but only to encourage her faith, I laughed and said, "Why don't you just do like I'm going to do? I don't have the money to pay the balance of my current tuition either, but I'm going to go ahead and register for next quarter."

"You can't do that!" she snapped. "They won't let you register for next quarter until your tuition for this quarter is paid."

"I know that," I said, "but it will be paid before I register."

"And where are you going to get the money?" she asked.

"I don't know where the money's going to come from," I responded, "but it'll be there when it's needed. The Lord will provide it."

If you were to look at the books in the registrar's office, you would have found that I owed $494.67 on my tuition at the time. I had $100.00 in the bank that I was going to put on it. I also had one check coming from my job which, after tithes and offerings, would leave me another balance of $100.00 to put on tuition. So, I actually needed only $294.67 in two weeks. No one knew the actual amount of my need except God and me.

A few days later, I received a letter from the office of financial aid. The letter indicated that it was the policy of that office to disburse unused grant monies at the end of each quarter on as equitable a basis as possible with some consideration for individual student needs. The office had decided to award me an additional $300.00 for the present quarter as well as an additional $300.00 for the next quarter. That would leave me a balance of $5.33 with which to celebrate!

This is just one instance of God's providential provision for me during my first two years in seminary. There were four other instances of such providential provision from unexpected sources that totaled $2,650. To keep the story honest, I must confess that I allowed the bug of materialism to bite me during my third year. I wanted a word processor so badly that I borrowed money to pay for it, thus compromising my biblical stance. After that, God's financial provision stopped flowing.

Over the next two years, my educational debt became a whopping $8,400! At the date of this writing, I've trimmed it to $1,700. I have since repented of the sin of materialism and have determined once again to live within my means while trusting God for the meeting of my needs.

While my last two years in school provided a hard lesson in the danger of materialism, the first two years taught me the biblical principle of prosperity. Kingdom priority produces kingdom provision. When we put God's kingdom first in our lives and are about our Father's business, we can expect him to provide for our needs so as to take care of our business.

We have seen that it is God's will for us that we prosper. We have come to understand the biblical principle for our prosperity. As we give priority in our lives *to* God's kingdom, we will receive provision for our needs *through* God's kingdom. Let's focus the discussion of biblical prosperity by defining our terms more specifically. What do we mean when we speak of prosperity? I believe that we can establish from the Lord's Prayer that petitioning God in prayer for our daily bread is to ask Him to meet both our basic needs and our higher needs. We prosper when all the needs of our lives are met.

Prosperity begins with the meeting of our basic needs. What do we petition God for? We ask him for "our daily bread" (Matthew 6:11). The down-to-earth character of this petition is enhanced by the term that is translated *daily*.(1) The term, in Greek, is *epiousios*. This word is found in Matthew's version of the Lord's Prayer, but nowhere else in the New Testament or in the entirety of Greek literature. One Greek church father, Origen, even went so far as to say that Matthew invented the word. When the Dead Sea scrolls were unearthed in 1947, however, a papyrus fragment was found that contained the word. The term *epiousios* appeared on a woman's shopping list as a category heading indicating items that needed to be purchased daily—items that were perishable and could spoil if stored in one's home for more than a day.

When we pray for God to give us our daily bread, we are literally acknowledging our dependence upon Him for the provision of our basic needs day by day. It is a prayer expressing trust in God for the basic essentials of everyday life.

Prosperity includes not only the meeting of our basic needs, but also the meeting of the higher needs of our lives—i.e., not only God's provision to sustain our physical lives but also His provision to sustain our spiritual lives. As Jesus stated elsewhere, "Man does not live on bread alone, but on every word that comes from the mouth of God" (Matthew 4:4).

That we should pray for the meeting of our higher needs is also communicated through this petition of the Lord's Prayer. This conclusion is based on the assumption that Matthew is using a literary device called *synecdoche.*(2) This literary device uses a part of something to represent the whole of it. So then, Jesus' reference to bread is understood not simply to refer to literal bread but also to everything necessary to sustain life. So then, implicit in this prayer is God's promise. That promise is stated by the Apostle Paul in this way: "And my God will meet *all your needs* according to his glorious riches in Christ Jesus" (Philippians 4:19, author's italics). The same promise is stated by the Apostle Peter in these words: "His divine power has given us *everything we need* for life and godliness through our knowledge of him who called us by his own glory and goodness" (2 Peter 1:3, author's italics).

Prosperity includes the meeting of both our basic needs and our higher needs. It includes not only provision for the sustaining of our bodies but also for the sustaining of our spirits. We may have all the creature comforts and luxuries that this world can afford and still be spiritually impoverished. Such a condition could hardly be called prosperity. It is in knowing and doing God's will that we truly prosper. John writes in his first general epistle, "The world and its desires pass away, but the man who does the will of God lives forever" (1 John 2:15).

Larry Lea tells of a personal acquaintance whose material wealth could not compensate for his spiritual impoverishment.(3) When Lea was a third year seminary student, he was invited by this well-to-do individual to have dinner at the elegant Petroleum Club of Fort Worth, Texas. After the blessing was said, Lea grabbed his fork and was ready to dig in. He stopped, though, when he noticed that his host was weeping. This distinguished, sixty-year-old millionaire still had his head bowed as the tears rolled onto his expensive silk tie.

Lea put his fork down and looked up at the gentleman. He said to him, "Sir, what's wrong? Can I help?" After the man got control of himself, he responded, "I was nineteen years old when God called me to preach, but I said no. I wanted my own way, wanted to make a lot of money. So I refused to take my hands off my life." He began to weep again. In a few seconds, he said in a broken voice, "But I don't have any peace. I missed God's purpose for my life."

To miss God's purpose for one's life is to miss out on prosperity. When we put God first, we are spiritually enriched and live with the assurance that God will provide for our material needs as well. Contrary to what Lea's acquaintance may have thought, God's will for his life would not have led him to poverty. God's will is to prosper His children on every level. John's wish for Gaius surely expresses God's will for all of His children: "Beloved, I wish above all things that thou mayest prosper and be in health, *even as thy soul prospereth*" (3 John 2, KJV, author's italics).

To summarize, when we pray the petition, "Give us this day our daily bread," we make an affirmation of faith. We affirm our faith that God's purpose is our prosperity. We affirm that it is not God's will that we be impoverished. It is, rather, His will that we be spiritually enriched and materially provided for. In praying this prayer, we are saying to God that as we have given priority in our lives *to* His kingdom so we expect provision for our needs *through* His kingdom.

God's Preconditions For Our Prosperity

God wants us to prosper. The biblical formula for prospering on God's terms is that kingdom priority produces kingdom provision. This implies that God has set preconditions for our prosperity. What are the preconditions for our prosperity? First, we must release hindrances to our prosperity. Second, we must embrace helps to our prosperity.

If we are to prosper on God's terms, we must release all hindrances to our prosperity. The Bible pinpoints two such hindrances that must be dealt with. They are our sins and our worldly attachments.

If we are to prosper, we must repent of our sins. We read in the book of Proverbs, "He who conceals his sins does not prosper, but whoever confesses and renounces them finds mercy" (28:13). We read also in John's epistle to Gaius, "Beloved, I wish above all things that thou mayest prosper and be in health, even as thy soul prospereth" (3 John 2, KJV). Both of these verses indicate that spiritual prosperity is the key to overall prosperity. When we understand this to be the case, we will not focus upon our material needs. We will learn to trust God to take care of them. Instead, we will focus upon our spiritual needs. We will endeavor to always keep a pure heart before God. We will sincerely repent of our sins.

If we are to prosper, we must not only repent of our sins. We must also release worldly attachments. This is not to say that those who have an abundance of this world's goods are, by virtue of that fact, disqualified from prospering in the biblical sense. God's blessing of prosperity upon the patriarchs of Israel made them men of enviable wealth. But our hearts must not be attached to our wealth. The problem with the rich young ruler who would not forsake his riches to follow Jesus was not that he was wealthy. Because his heart was attached to his wealth, he was unable to pursue a course that would make him spiritually prosperous. Jesus said to His disciples about this man and those like him, "Children, how hard it is *for those who trust in riches* to enter the kingdom of God!" (Mark 10:24; author's italics). The measure of our prosperity is not the measure of our material wealth. Rather, our prosperity or lack of it depends upon the allegiance of our hearts. If our hearts are to be devoted to God and his kingdom, we must release all worldly attachments that would compete for our loyalty.

To prosper on God's terms, we must not only release hindrances to our prosperity. We must also embrace helps to our prosperity. The Bible emphasizes two such helps to prosperity. We must be both diligent in labor and faithful in liberality.

If we are to prosper, we must be diligent in labor. It will not do to think that God will bless us with the supply of all of our needs while we neglect responsibility for our own provision. We must contribute toward our own material well-being. Solomon says, "Lazy hands make a man poor, but diligent hands bring wealth" (Proverbs10:4). This is not just the wisdom of the Old Testament. Hear these words of Paul addressed to the Christians in Thessalonica:

> Make it your ambition to lead a quiet life, to mind your own business and to work with your hands, just as we told you, so that your daily life may win the respect of outsiders and so that you will not be dependent on anybody—1 Thessalonians 4:11,12.

Biblical prosperity clearly includes financial independence and, therefore, requires that we be diligent in labor.

Another help to our prosperity is that we be faithful in liberality. The Bible teaches that the degree of our prosperity in the material realm is determined by the degree of our liberality in giving. In this connection, we will comment on two biblical principles concerning our giving. They are, namely, the principle of the tithe and the principle of reciprocity.

We cannot prosper unless we tithe. This was the message of Malachi to those Jews who returned to their homeland after the Babylonian exile was over. God spoke through the prophet Malachi and said to these Jews, "You are under a curse—the whole nation of you—because you are robbing me" (3:9). How were they robbing God? God's answer was that they were doing so by withholding their tithes and their offerings. (See verse 8.) Those who don't tithe—that is, those who don't give ten percent of their income to God—are judged by God to be thieves. God says they are under a curse. They cannot prosper. God's word to them is not a word of judgment, but of exhortation. He says:

> "Bring the whole tithe into the storehouse, that there may be food in my house. Test me in this," says the Lord Almighty, "and see if I will not throw open the floodgates of heaven and pour out so much blessing that you will not have room enough for it. I will prevent pests from devouring your crops, and the vines in your fields will not cast their fruit," says the Lord Almighty—Malachi 3:10,11.

Tithing is a necessary means to biblical prosperity. God expects us to tithe no matter how small our income or how great our need. For in tithing, we are supporting the work of God's kingdom. When we give priority to God's kingdom, God will meet our needs. Remember, kingdom priority produces kingdom provision.

Pat Robertson relates a story that illustrates the priority that God gives to tithing as a means toward the prosperity of His people.(4) A missionary to Chile tells of a pastor whose congregation consisted of peasants. At his own expense, this godly, caring man faithfully shepherded these poor people. He taught them God's Word on many important aspects of Christian living. He taught them about salvation, the Spirit-filled life, and receiving miracles from God. He taught them to live holy lives as they expectantly looked for the Second Coming of Christ.

One day, this pastor was in prayer when God spoke to him. God reproved him for not having declared the entire counsel of Scripture to his congregation. When he asked God to tell him what area of biblical teaching he had neglected to teach, the Lord said to him, "You have not declared My tithe." This missionary pastor complained, "But Lord, these are very poor people! They hardly have enough to live on. I can't ask them to tithe. They have nothing." Nonetheless, God's word to him was resolute. The Lord responded, "You must declare to them My tithe."

The following Sunday, this pastor obeyed the Lord. He led his congregation in an hour-long discourse from the Scriptures concerning God's command that His people tithe and God's promise to prosper those who do. The people listened attentively and resolved to take the message to heart.

The following weeks, these peasants brought their tithes to church. They did not have money, so they brought chickens, eggs, woven articles and leather goods. The altar was filled with their gifts. The pastor sold the goods and used the money discreetly. He spent some on church work, some on benevolences to the destitute in the community and kept some as his salary.

Shortly afterwards, God proved His word to these people. A drought swept over the countryside of such severity that crops began to fail and buildings deteriorate. But those who belonged to this church received God's miraculous provision. Their crops produced record yields and were preserved from pests; their livestock remained strong and healthy and their fields flourished while the effects of drought raged all around them. It wasn't long before their offerings included money, and they were able to build a much more adequate meeting place for the church to the glory of God.

Robertson concludes this story with these words: "Despite his misgivings, the missionary and his people had learned that no matter how desperate the situation, no matter how deep the impoverishment, the principles of the kingdom can turn deprivation into abundance."(5)

There are many Christians who complain that they cannot afford to tithe. Such individuals fail to understand two things. First, tithing is not an option—God commands it. Second, tithing is a means to prosperity. When we obey God in the tithe, we open the door for God to providentially provide for us by meeting our needs. If we don't tithe, we tie God's hands so that He cannot prosper us as He desires to.

Faithfulness in liberality *begins* with tithing. Tithing itself is a duty. It is required of us by God. Therefore, it is not an indication of liberality. But it is the beginning of liberality since we must fulfill our duty before we can surpass it. Therefore, tithing is a help to our prosperity.

To be faithful in liberality, we must surpass the tithe and embrace the biblical principle of reciprocity. This principle is stated in these words of Jesus: "Give, and it will be given to you. A good measure, pressed down, shaken together and running over, will be poured into your lap. For with the measure you use, it will be measured to you" (Luke 6:38). Paul expresses the same truth in these words penned to the Corinthians: "Whoever sows sparingly will also reap sparingly, and whoever sows generously will also reap generously" (2 Corinthians 9:6). God's liberality in providing for us is in direct proportion to our liberality in giving. When we understand this to be the case, we will not be legalistic givers but cheerful givers.

The world's philosophy of prosperity can be stated this way: "Get all you can, can all you get and sit on the can." God's principle of prosperity is quite opposite: "Give generously and cheerfully and you will receive abundantly."

God's Plan For Our Prosperity

Once we know that it is God's purpose for us to prosper, and once we have met God's preconditions for our prosperity, we are ready to commit ourselves to God's plan for our prosperity. And what is that plan? It is threefold. First, we must learn to look to Him in faith to be the source of all that we need to sustain our lives. Second, we must obey when God has shown us the part that we are to play in the meeting of our needs. Third, we must petition God for the meetings of our needs with childlike trust and relentless persistence.

First, we must learn to look to God in faith to meet our needs. If we are to look to God in faith to prosper us, we must have an accurate perspective of God's part in our prosperity. We must learn, as is popularly stated, that God is our source of supply. Meeting the preconditions for prosperity does not *earn* us God's blessings. It merely puts us in a place where we are able to receive His blessings.

Paul Yonggi Cho tells of an English couple whom he helped to gain an accurate perspective of God's part in their prosperity.(6) Cho was holding a revival in a small town in England. A couple in the church invited him to their home for dinner. After dining, the woman of the house informed him that she had invited him over for a reason. She and her husband were having great financial problems and needed counsel. They had worked very hard in various business ventures to support themselves. But all their efforts had failed. They had accumulated a large debt just to subsist. They were so worried about the growing debt that they had lost their appetite and could hardly sleep at night. They had even put their home up for sale but could not seem to find a buyer.

Cho discerned that this couple was guilty of not trusting God to provide for them. They were trying to do their part and God's, too. So, after the woman finished describing the problem, Cho had her get her Bible and open to the Genesis account of creation. He walked with her through each day of creation to illustrate God's role in providing for His people. He pointed out that God created the entire universe, the earth and everything on the earth before He created humankind. After He had created humankind, He declared His work finished and He rested.

Cho explained to this woman that Adam and Eve did not need to provide anything for themselves. God had already provided everything they would need. All that was required of them was that they trust Him, obey Him and be thankful. This is the way God intended for His people to prosper. Cho told her that she and her husband were worrying about their basic needs and the selling of their house when such concerns are God's responsibility toward His children. They were trying to do God's job. Thus they were hindering God's blessing in their lives.

The English woman accepted Cho's words with humility and appreciation. When her husband got home from work, she related Cho's message to him as well. He also humbly received it as God's word to them. The two of them prayed together, asked God's forgiveness for their lack of trust and gave thanks to God for meeting their needs. A few days later, their home was sold at a price far higher than they had asked. They were able to move into a smaller but very elegant home. They had gained an accurate perspective of God's part in their prosperity.

Once we have met God's preconditions for prosperity as we have already discussed them, we must learn to trust God and thank Him for taking care of our needs. We must learn to gratefully let Him be our God and provider. When we do so, we will have God's perspective for our prosperity.

Second, if we are to prosper on God's terms, we must obey God when he shows us the part that we are to play in the meeting of our needs. Such obedience also requires trust in the promises of God.

The children of Israel learned early on in their wilderness wanderings that they would have to trust and obey God if they were to experience His provision for the meeting of their needs. (See Exodus 16:1-30.) God taught them this lesson in the way He provided their food. He rained bread from heaven in the mornings and sent quail down upon the wilderness floor in the evenings. Through Moses, He instructed the people that they were to gather up the bread every day and not keep any till the next day. On the sixth day of the week, they were to gather enough for two days so that they would not need to work on the Sabbath. Some ignored God's instructions and kept the bread in their tents overnight during the week. Invariably, bread kept overnight became infested with maggots and gave off a foul odor. Others ignored God's word and went out on the Sabbath to gather bread only to find that there was none. Thus they learned that they would have to trust God and obey Him if they were to enjoy His blessing of provision for their needs. God was teaching them to look to Him for literal daily bread.

Oftentimes, Christians can fall into the trap of practical atheism. By practical atheism, I mean believing in God, having a personal relationship with Jesus Christ and yet living as though there is no God. We are practical atheists when we don't look to God to meet our needs but think that we must assume sole responsibility for our own welfare. This is the mistake of Christians who become workoholics in order to raise their own support. They are always trying to get ahead in the fear of getting behind. If God sends them manna for one day, they scramble to gather enough for two days. If God tells them to take a vacation and get some needed rest, they excitedly welcome the bosses offer to put in overtime at time-and-a-half pay. Such people need to learn the lesson that God taught the Israelites in the wilderness. They must learn to assume the posture for prosperity—a posture characterized by trusting God's benevolence and obeying God's commands.

Third, God's plan for our prosperity is that we petition Him in prayer for the meeting of our needs. The Bible says, "You do not have, because you do not ask God" (James 4:2). How are we to petition God for the meeting of our needs? We are to petition Him with childlike trust and relentless persistence.

We are to pray, "Give us today our daily bread" with childlike trust. Such trust is exemplified in the prayer life of George Muller.(7) Muller established orphanages in Bristol, England during the nineteenth century. The orphanages cared for several hundred children at a time. Yet Muller had no support base and did not go out to raise funds. He simply prayed and trusted God to provide for the needs of the children. And God always did.

One morning, there was no milk for the children's breakfast. Muller had all the children sit around the tables and join him in prayer for their heavenly Father to provide them with milk for breakfast. Suddenly a knock came at the door. A milk cart that was making deliveries had broken down just outside the orphanage. The driver asked that the orphanage take the milk and use it as it would spoil by the time the cart could be repaired. Muller had successfully taught the children to petition God for the meeting of their daily needs and to offer their petitions with simple trust in God. We must do the same.

Not only are we to pray, "Give us today our daily bread" with childlike trust. We also must pray this petition with relentless persistence. This is clearly taught through the context of the Lord's Prayer in Luke's gospel. There, Jesus' account of the Lord's Prayer is followed by a parable emphasizing persistence in petitioning for bread

(11:5-8). It is about a man who had guests arrive in the middle of the night. As he had no food to set before them, he went to his neighbor's house, knocked at his door and boldly requested three loaves of bread. The neighbor, still in bed, refused at first to help him. Because the man kept knocking and would not take no for an answer, the neighbor dragged himself out of bed and provided the three loaves that were requested. Jesus closed the parable with instruction to His disciples to persist in prayer for the basic necessities of life in faith that God would hear their prayers and give them the good things they ask for. (11:9-13.)

Now, it's interesting that Jesus taught us to petition God for our daily bread in simple childlike faith *and* with persistence. These two approaches seem to be contradictory. But when we remember that the kingdom of God must be taken by force, then we understand that even our persistence is in faith. That is, we reach out in faith to take what God freely gives us but what Satan tries to withhold from us. God allows the struggle not because He begrudges us His blessings of provision. Rather, He allows the struggle in order that our faith may be tested, tried and strengthened. Thus in securing what prospers our bodies, we endure a process that will work in us true spiritual prosperity.

Summing It Up

God desires to prosper all of His children. We ask God for the blessing of divine prosperity every time we pray, "Give us today our daily bread" (Matthew 6:11). But in order to pray this petition in faith and receive the answer to our prayer, we must understand God's purpose for our prosperity, meet His prerequisites for our prosperity, and abide by His plan for our prosperity.

God's purpose for our prosperity is that all our needs be met spiritually and materially. It is in prospering spiritually that we come to prosper materially. Kingdom priority produces kingdom provision.

God's prerequisites for our prosperity are the removal of hindrances and the employment of helps to prosperity. We must remove from our hearts hindrances to our own well-being such as sins for which we have not truly repented and worldly attachments that would steal the allegiance of our hearts away from true devotion to God. We must embrace such helps as diligence in labor and faithfulness in liberality. As for the latter, we must obey God by tithing in order to open the door for God's blessings upon us. Beyond the tithe, the measure of our liberality in giving determines the measure to which God can prosper us.

Finally, God's plan for our prosperity is that we trust Him to provide for our needs, obey Him in assuming our responsibility toward the provision of our needs, and petition Him for the meeting of our needs with childlike trust and relentless persistence. Abiding by this plan is essential to receiving the blessing of divine prosperity.

As we take this word to heart, we will experience prosperity at every level of our lives on God's terms rather than our own. Thus our lives will glorify God and promote His kingdom.

Notes

1. From *The Gospel of Matthew*, (Volume I: The Daily Study Bible Series) (Revised Edition), by William Barclay. Copyright © 1975 William Barclay. Used by permission of Westminster/John Knox Press and Saint Andrew Press, p. 194; see also R. T. France, *Matthew* (Leicester and Grand Rapids: InterVarsity Press and William B. Eerdmans Publishing Company, 1985), p. 132.

2. Everett L. Fullam with Bob Slosser, *Living The Lord's Prayer* (Old Tappan, New Jersey: Fleming H. Revell Company, 1980), pp. 92,93.

3. Used by permission of Creation House, Lake Mary, Florida, from *Could You Not Tarry One Hour?* by Larry Lea. Copyright © 1987, p. 103.

4. Pat Robertson with Bob Slosser, *The Secret Kingdom* (Nashville: Thomas Nelson Publishers, 1982), pp. 109-111.

5. Ibid., p. 111.

6. Used by permission of Creation House, Altamonte Springs, Florida, from *Praying With Jesus* by Paul Yonggi Cho. Copyright © 1987, pp. 62-67.

7. Anna Talbott McPherson, *They Dared To Be Different* (Chicago: Moody Press, 1967), pp. 171-173.

Chapter Six

Kingdom Pardon

Forgive us our debts, as we also have forgiven our debtors. . . . For if you forgive men when they sin against you, your heavenly Father will also forgive you. But if you do not forgive men their sins, your Father will not forgive your sins.
—Matthew 6:11,14,15

There is an axiom about forgiveness that is both familiar and profound. The axiom says, "To err is human; to forgive, divine." This saying might lead one to the inaccurate conclusion that a person would have to be divine in order to forgive. This would mean that only God is capable of forgiving an offender. But there is another way of interpreting this saying. To forgive is divine because one cannot truly and completely forgive another unless he is enabled by God to do so. In the words of James Bjorge,

"The one who forgives us empowers us to forgive others."(1) In this light, all forgiveness is divine.

When we pray for the coming of God's kingdom, we are asking that God be born in us and reign in us. God living and reigning in us gives us the power to forgive others in the same manner and degree as He forgives us. Since the kingdom of God in us empowers us to forgive, our forgiveness of others is aptly called kingdom pardon.

In this chapter, we will focus upon the petition of the Lord's Prayer that concerns forgiveness and the verses immediately following the Lord's Prayer which underscore and reinforce the point of this petition. (See Matthew 6:11,14,15.) Using these verses as the basis of our discussion, we will endeavor to learn how to forgive others divinely through kingdom pardon. In doing so, we will speak first about the *meaning* of forgiveness and then about the *measure* of forgiveness.

The Meaning Of Forgiveness

First let's examine the *meaning* of forgiveness. This might seem unnecessary to some as the concept of forgiveness is familiar to everyone. But people who claim to know what forgiveness means often understand it in a way that is vague and misleading. When people affirm their belief that God has forgiven their sins and yet continue to feel guilty over specific sins of the past, they demonstrate an inaccurate concept of forgiveness. When people express forgiveness to others for personal offenses but avow that they will never forget the offenses, they demonstrate an inaccurate concept of forgiveness. Because of the prevalence of these human tendencies to condemn oneself and to bear grudges against others, it is necessary that we re-examine our understanding of forgiveness.

What does it mean to forgive? Webster defines the term as meaning "to pardon; to cease to bear resentment against; to cancel (as a debt)."(2) From this definition, we conclude that forgiveness has both a legal aspect and a personal aspect. The *legal* aspect of forgiveness is communicated by the reference to pardoning a person by canceling a debt. It is to release a person from all obligations incurred by an offense that would make him indebted to us. It is to give him, in legal terms, a clear record. The *personal* aspect of forgiveness is communicated by the reference to the cessation of resentment against the offender. It is to release a person from the ill-will that has resulted from an offense. Thus forgiveness restores broken relationships.

We've seen what forgiveness means in modern English usage. But what does it mean in biblical usage? What does it mean in the mouth of our Lord in the Lord's Prayer? John Wesley points out that Jesus' formulation of the petition concerning forgiveness communicates two ideas: the cancellation of a debt and the loosing of a chain.(3) This analysis makes Jesus' teaching on forgiveness fully consonant with the meaning of forgiveness as used in modern English. In speaking of forgiveness as the cancellation of debt, Jesus emphasized the legal aspect of forgiveness by which an offender's record is cleared. As for the image of the loosing of a chain, this speaks of the personal aspect of forgiveness. It portrays the offender as being loosed from the bondage of ill-will and restored to favor with those whom he has offended.

It should be clear by now that forgiveness not only pardons the offender but removes the offense. In fact, the very word that Jesus used that is rendered "forgive" literally means "to send away."(4) The offense by which a person becomes morally indebted to God or to others is cleared from his record, lifted from his life and sent away. In practical terms, this means that one who believes God has forgiven his sins must release all guilt for past sins. It means that one who forgives another who has offended him must forget the offense itself. True forgiveness leaves no place for resentment on the part of the offended or guilt on the part of the offender. The offense itself has been sent away.

When we pray, "Forgive us our debts, as we also have forgiven our debtors" (Matthew 6:12), we speak of forgiveness on the vertical plane of our relationship with God and on the horizontal plane of our relationship with others. To truly grasp the meaning of forgiveness, we must understand how to receive forgiveness from God and how to give it to others.

Receiving forgiveness from God is illustrated in a helpful way in the Old Testament system of atonement for sin. We read about it in Leviticus 16. On the day of atonement, the nation of Israel offered two male goats for a sin offering. The officiating priest slaughtered one of the goats and offered its blood to atone for the sins of the people (vs. 9,15-19). The other goat is referred to as "the scapegoat" or "the goat of removal" (vs. 8 and NIV footnote). The priest laid his hands upon the head of this live goat and confessed the sins of the Israelite community upon it. This scapegoat was then taken out of the Israelite community and sent away into the desert (vs. 20-22). The offenses of the people were visibly sent away.

This Old Testament practice teaches us much about how to receive from God the forgiveness of our sins. Two thousand years ago, God took all of our sins—past, present and future—and laid them upon Christ at the cross. (See 1 Peter 2:24.) Through His substitutionary death, Jesus bore our sins away. Thus Jesus became our scapegoat. When Jesus died for our sins, our sins died with Him. Furthermore, through His resurrection, Jesus conquered the effects of sin on our behalf. Now, through personal faith in the atoning work of Christ's death on our behalf, we can rejoice in the promise of Scripture, "....as far as the east is from the west, so far has he removed our transgressions from us" (Psalm 103:12).

How do we receive from God the forgiveness of our sins? We simply embrace by faith in Christ the twofold blessing of pardon and remission. When we do, both the guilt of our sin and the sin itself are removed from us. We are restored in our relationship with God.

We receive from God the forgiveness of our sins by faith in the atoning sacrifice of Christ alone. If thoughts of past sins come back to our minds and our hearts begin to be troubled, we can set ourselves at ease by the assurance that our forgiveness is not conditioned upon our thoughts and feelings—it is conditioned only upon our faith in God's grace freely given to us through Christ.

James Bjorge relates a hypothetical story that suggests how to hold fast to our forgiveness when voices from the past attempt to trouble the waters of our hearts.(5) Imagine a man who is renting a house from a harsh and greedy landlord. The landlord charges him an unreasonably high rent and penalizes him when his payments are late. Yet, when repairs need to be made, the landlord keeps putting him off.

One day, a stranger knocks at the door and presents legal documents indicating that he has bought the house. The new landlord informs the occupant that he may now live in the house free of rent. The occupant can scarcely believe it. But he has seen the evidence and knows that it is so. He graciously thanks the stranger and gratefully accepts the offer.

A couple of weeks later, the old landlord knocks on the door and demands his rent. What will the occupant do? Will he allow the old landlord to talk him into paying a debt he doesn't owe? Of course not! Will he argue with the old landlord? No! He'll simply say, "Take up your problem with the new landlord."

When we affirm in faith that our sins are forgiven for Christ's sake, voices from the past will try to haunt us. Whether those voices come through our own recollection of past offenses or whether they come from others who will not forgive us, they are all inspired by our old master, the devil. When we recognize him as the culprit, we won't need to bow to his reason and continue to pay on our sin debt through guilt. Nor will there be any reason to argue with him in an effort to see who will win the debate. We can simply shrug him off by saying, "Take up your problem with my new master, Jesus!" This is a sure and effective way to stand fast in our assurance of God's grace and forgiveness.

We have discussed the manner in which we receive forgiveness of sins from God. We acknowledge that our sins were laid upon Christ at the cross, borne away through His death, and forever conquered through His resurrection. Through faith in His blood atonement, we receive both pardon and remission with the result that we can now live free from guilt and condemnation. Now we turn to consider the flip side of the coin of forgiveness. Just as it is important that we understand how to *receive* forgiveness of our sins from God, it is important also that we know how to *give* forgiveness to our offenders.

During my teens, I heard noted Bible teacher Marilyn Hickey speak on the subject of forgiveness. As she talked about the need to forgive others, she employed an interesting teaching tool to aid the listeners in understanding how offenses develop and how we can release offenses and truly forgive those who have hurt us. Let's consider first the growth of an offense and then the way of forgiveness.

How do offenses grow? When someone says or does something to us to hurt us, we can either respond graciously or we can turn it into an offense. We turn it into an offense in three stages. First, we *curse* it. We express our anger against the person who has attacked us and speak vengeful words against him. Then we *nurse* it. By constantly thinking about it, we coddle it and feed it so that it grows bigger than life. Then we *rehearse* it. We re-enact the event in our minds in technicolor and edit it so that we come out looking better each time. Thus we have taken a hurt and made it into an offense.

This is how offenses grow. But how do we find the grace to truly forgive the offender so that the offense is, as we've seen, lifted from our lives and sent away? We have a part to play in forgiveness, and God has a part to play. Our part is in giving the offense to God and totally releasing it into His hands. We must *disperse* it. We must truly humble ourselves, repent, let go of the offense and trust God to handle the situation in His wisdom. When we do, God will *reverse* it. As we release God to deal with the person's heart directly about the offense, we will experience spiritual growth through the situation.

Marilyn Hickey's scheme is very beneficial in helping us to understand how to give forgiveness to others in that it emphasizes a God-centered approach to forgiveness. Forgiveness is not simply letting go of an offense. It is, rather, giving the offense to God. It expresses implicit trust in God to deal with the situation so as to bring the offender around while enabling us to grow in our trust in God's wisdom and goodness. Thus we come to understand that to forgive another is an act of love toward that person and an expression of trust in God. It is kingdom pardon.

The Measure Of Forgiveness

We have discussed the meaning of forgiveness and seen how a proper understanding of forgiveness bears upon our receiving forgiveness from God and our giving forgiveness to others. While our text does effectively lead us into a more accurate understanding of forgiveness, it further emphasizes the importance of the *measure* to which forgiveness is either given or received. In order to tap into this more central point of the text, we turn now to talk about the measure of forgiveness.

Jesus commissions us to pray, "Forgive us our debts, as we also have forgiven our debtors" (Matthew 6:12). To make sure we understand the connection between the forgiveness we receive and the forgiveness we give, Jesus returns to this matter in the verses immediately following the Lord's Prayer. He says, "For if you forgive men when they sin against you, your heavenly Father will also forgive you. But if you do not forgive their sins, your Father will not forgive your sins" (Matthew 6:14,15).

These verses teach us that forgiveness works according to a principle of reciprocity. Only as we give forgiveness to others who have offended us will we receive forgiveness of our sins from God. This principle of reciprocity is effectively communicated by paraphrases of the petition concerning forgiveness as provided by William Barclay and Everett Fullam. Barclay paraphrases the petition to read, "Forgive us our sins *in proportion* as we forgive those who have sinned against us."(6) Fullam's paraphrase makes the point even more pungently: "Father, forgive my sins *only* to the extent I am willing to forgive those who have sinned against me."(7) Clearly, God's forgiveness of us is contingent upon our forgiveness of others.

The principle of reciprocity in forgiveness can be used for our good or for our harm. First, it can be used for our good. All of us want God's mercy in the forgiveness of our sins. But how do we receive God's mercy? The answer comes to us through the beatitude, "Blessed are the merciful, for they will be shown mercy" (Matthew 5:7). As we are merciful to others, we open the door for God to be merciful to us. In the words of James, "Mercy triumphs over judgment!" (2:13). Second, the principle of reciprocity in forgiveness can be used for our harm. John Wesley pointed out that to pray the petition of the Lord's Prayer concerning forgiveness without having forgiven those who have wronged us is "to come before God in open defiance. We are daring Him to do His worst."(8) In the words of James, " . . . judgment without mercy will be shown to anyone who has not been merciful" (2:13). To refuse to forgive those who have wronged us is to choose to live under God's wrath rather than in His favor.

Understanding what the Bible teaches us about the measure of forgiveness enables us to learn a valuable lesson about human nature. To begrudge another person is to put oneself in bondage. To forgive another person is to set oneself at liberty. Let's consider each of these assertions.

First of all, to hold a grudge against another person is to put oneself in bondage. Jesus said, "Do not judge, or you too will be judged. For in the same way you judge others, you will be judged, and with the measure you use, it will be measured to you" (Matthew 7:1,2). I believe this passage gives us insight into the working principle of the human conscience. To pass judgment upon others is to invite our conscience to pass the very same judgment upon us.

Paul Yonggi Cho relates a helpful illustration here.(9) During the administration of President Andrew Jackson, a man named George Wilson witnessed a thief stealing something of value from a U. S. post office. In vengeance, Wilson shot the man to death. The authorities arrested Wilson, and he was brought to trial and sentenced with capital punishment. President Jackson reviewed the case, however, and issued a pardon that officially acquitted Mr. Wilson and discharged him from his incarceration.

Mr. Wilson was a free man! Or was he? His conscience would not allow him to accept the pardon. Because of the uncertainties attached to the unprecedented instance of a capital offender rejecting a presidential pardon, the case was eventually appealed to the Supreme Court. Justice John Marshall gave this statement:

> The letter of pardon is merely a piece of paper, but it has the power to pardon as long as the person who is the object of pardon accepts it. If the person who is the object of pardon refused to accept it, he cannot be acquitted. Therefore, the death penalty sentenced to George Wilson should be carried out.

The case of George Wilson is a warning to us. If we are not merciful to others but condemn them, our consciences will in turn condemn us. But when we are merciful toward others regardless of their offense against us, we will have a clear conscience toward God.

If holding a grudge against another person is to put oneself in bondage, then to forgive an offender is to set oneself at liberty. It is living in love that breaks the power of sin in our own lives.

To live in love is to forgive unconditionally. It is to forgive abundantly. It is not to ask with Peter, "Lord, how many times shall I forgive my brother when he sins against me? Up to seven times?" (Matthew 18:21). Rather, it is to submit to Jesus command, "I tell you, not seven times, but seventy-seven times" (vs. 22). That is, we are to forgive every offense against us. And we are to forgive abundantly. We are to forgive like God forgives.

God forgives us abundantly. This is communicated to us through the parable of the prodigal son. (See Luke 15:11-32.) When the prodigal had wasted all of his share of his father's estate in extravagant living, he devised a plan to press himself back into his father's service as a hired hand. He wasn't sure his father would receive him even in this capacity after he had so ruined the family name and wasted his father's hard-earned living. But as he made his way back home with an empty stomach, a heavy heart and a trembling form, his father saw him in the distance. Would his father forgive him? He forgave him abundantly! He ran to his son, embraced him and kissed him. In his joy to have his son back home again, he ordered the servants to adorn him with the best robe in the house, with a ring for his finger and sandals for his feet. Would his father forgive him? He forgave him abundantly! He ordered, "Bring the fattened calf and kill it. Let's have a feast and celebrate. For this son of mine was dead and is alive again; he was lost and is found" (Luke 15:23,24).

We have all been prodigal sons and daughters. But God has forgiven us abundantly through the grace of our Lord Jesus Christ. Because He has, we are to forgive others abundantly. We are not simply to relieve a person who has offended us from any sense of indebtedness to us. Nor are we to stop at letting go of any feelings of resentment that we have had toward the person. We are to aim at a restored relationship with the person concerned so that we celebrate the reconciliation. This is what it means to forgive abundantly.

James Bjorge relates a wonderful illustration of abundant forgiveness.(10) The story is told by a prison warden from the Old West of an elderly man who was sitting next to a tense young man on a train. As they were talking, the young man told of how he had gotten in trouble with the law and wound up in prison. His family was disgraced by the news to the point that all communication between the family and him had ceased. Now that his prison sentence was up, he was returning home in the hopes that his family would forgive him and receive him. Before leaving the prison, he had written a letter to his family telling them that he would be coming home by train. In the letter, he asked them to hang a white ribbon on the apple tree by the railroad track if they forgave him and would welcome him home. If he didn't see a white ribbon on the tree, he would go on his way and never bother them again.

As the train began to pass familiar landmarks approaching his family's farm, the young man became so emotionally distraught that he couldn't bear to watch. He asked the older man to watch for him. As the apple tree came into view, the man put his hand on the boy's shoulder and said happily, "It's all right! The whole tree is white with ribbons!" Bjorge closes the story with the assuring affirmation, "The apple tree spoke the language of heaven."

The key to genuine forgiveness is abundant love. For abundant love produces abundant forgiveness. When we love as God loves, we will forgive as God forgives. Our forgiving of others who have offended us is none other than kingdom pardon.

Summing It Up

As we have been born into God's family through faith in Jesus Christ, we have become citizens of God's kingdom. The result is that we have been abundantly pardoned by God's grace and received freely into God's favor. It is now incumbent upon us to witness to the presence of God's kingdom among men by abundantly pardoning those who would offend us through kingdom pardon. We witness to the presence of the kingdom of God when we show the world that to forgive is divine.

To forgive others through kingdom pardon, we must be clear on the meaning of forgiveness. It entails both releasing others from any indebtedness to us and releasing all ill feelings against them. We must also understand the measure of forgiveness that is truly reflective of kingdom pardon. We must forgive abundantly and welcome the offender back into harmonious relationship. We must celebrate every reconciliation with sincere joy.

God's Word empowers us to forgive by reminding us that the key to forgiveness is abundant love—the love God gives to us through Christ that is shed abroad in our hearts by the Holy Spirit. (See Romans 5:5.) As we live in submission to God's kingdom reign in us, we will find that God's forgiveness of us empowers us to forgive others wholeheartedly. Our feeble human efforts at forgiveness will be transformed into the joyous celebration characteristic of kingdom pardon.

Notes

1. Reprinted from *Living in the Forgiveness of God* by James R. Bjorge, Copyright © 1990 Augsburg Fortress. Used by permission, p. 66.

2. John Gage Agee, ed., *Webster's Encyclopedia of Dictionaries* (U.S.A.: Ottenheimer Publishers, Inc., 1958), p. 152.

3. John Wesley, *The Nature of the Kingdom,* Edited and updated by Clare George Weakley, Jr. (Minneapolis: Bethany House Publishers, 1979), p. 161.

4. W. E. Vine, "An Expository Dictionary of New Testament Words," in *Vine's Expository Dictionary of Biblical Words,* by W. E. Vine, Merrill F. Unger and William White (Nashville: Thomas Nelson Publishers, 1985), p. 250.

5. Bjorge, pp. 52-53.

6. From *The Gospel of Matthew,* (Volume I: The Daily Study Bible Series) (Revised Edition), by William Barclay. Copyright © 1975 William Barclay. Used by permission of Westminster/John Knox Press and Saint Andrew Press, p. 222.

7. Everett Fullam with Bob Slosser, *Living the Lord's Prayer* (Old Tappan, New Jersey: Fleming H. Revell Company, 1980), p.109.

8. Wesley, p. 162.

9. Used by permission of Creation House, Altamonte Springs, Florida, from *Praying With Jesus* by Paul Yonggi Cho, Copyright © 1987, p. 79.

10. Bjorge, p. 77.

Chapter Seven

Kingdom Protection

And lead us not into temptation, but deliver us from the evil one. . . . .—Matthew 6:13a.

Much can be learned about a person's perception of life by reading the plaques he hangs upon the walls of his home or office and the bumper stickers with which he decorates his car. In the process of writing a book about temptation, Charles Stanley's attention was drawn within a short time to both a plaque and a bumper sticker relevant to his subject. The plaque read, "OPPORTUNITY ONLY KNOCKS ONCE, TEMPTATION LEANS ON THE DOORBELL."(1) The bumper sticker read, "LEAD ME NOT INTO TEMPTATION, I CAN FIND IT MYSELF."(2)

Both these statements communicate a common truth about temptation that Christians especially must acknowledge. While we have been set free from the power of sin and are not obliged any longer to be its slaves (see Romans 6:11,12), we have not been delivered from the power of temptation that appeals to our desires in an effort to lead us back into sin. (See Galatians 5:17.) This very fact accounts for Jesus' prayer for the saints in all ages, "My prayer is not that you take them out of the world but that you protect them from the evil one" (John 17:15). God does not lead us to a life free of temptations. Rather, He teaches us how to look to Him for the necessary strength with which to deal with temptation appropriately.

Temptation is a fact of life. No matter how Christ-like we become, there will always be areas of weakness and vulnerability in which we are tempted to succumb to evil. These weak spots keep us humbly aware of our dependence upon God to be our strength and our shield of protection.

Jesus instructs us to pray, "And lead us not into temptation, but deliver us from the evil one" (Matthew 6:13). This petition amounts to an admission that we cannot overcome temptation in our own power. Temptation is not to be fought with human willpower. It is not a test of our willpower at all. It is a test of our faith. (See James 1:3.) Therefore, the way to resist temptation is to lean heavily upon God's grace to strengthen us and enable us to stand against the wiles of the devil. Only God can preserve us from testings that would overpower us. Only God can save us from the evil one who would devour us. When we look to God in prayer to grant us the grace and strength necessary to withstand temptation, we are appealing to our King for kingdom protection.

God gives us kingdom protection from the ill-effects of temptation and the ill-will of the tempter when we pray with Jesus, "Lead us not into temptation, but deliver us from the evil one" (Matthew 6:13). In answer to this prayer God protects us from the dangers of temptation by enabling us to:

1. understand temptation
2. face temptation
3. endure temptation
4. overcome temptation

Understanding Temptation

The first way in which God grants us kingdom protection against the ill-effects of temptation and the ill-will of the tempter is by enabling us to *understand* temptation. We must begin our discussion of this petition of the Lord's Prayer by endeavoring to understand just what temptation is all about. The need for such understanding is readily apparent when we consider that the word temptation has a narrower meaning in modern English than it did in 1611 when the King James translators provided us with the Authorized Version of the Bible. Today, we use the word temptation to mean *enticement*. This is in accord with Webster who defines the term as "inducement to do evil."(3) This negative aspect of temptation is often characteristic of the use of the word in the Bible. (See Luke 4:2 and James 1:14.) But the Bible also uses the word with positive connotations. In Scripture, to tempt a person may mean to "try" or "test" him in order to determine his strengths, weaknesses and loyalties with a view to bringing him to greater maturity. (See Genesis 22:1 and Hebrews 2:18.)

When we understand that the Bible uses the word temptation in both its negative and its positive aspects, we can avoid confusion over apparent inconsistencies in Scripture and come to a more accurate understanding of what the Bible teaches about temptation. One seeming inconsistency is much cited. James warns against accusing God of tempting men. He writes: "When tempted, no one should say, `God is tempting me.' For God cannot be tempted by evil, nor does he tempt anyone" (1:13). On the other hand, we read that God "tempted" Abraham in commanding him to offer his son, Isaac, as a burnt offering upon an altar at Mount Moriah. (See Genesis 22:1, KJV.) What appears to be a contradiction is resolved when we understand that God was not maliciously enticing Abraham to evil but was simply testing Abraham's loyalty to his God.

This brief analysis of the biblical connotations of the word temptation enables us to interpret this petition of the Lord's Prayer. Jesus said we should pray, saying, "And lead us not into temptation, but deliver us from the evil one" (Matthew 6:13). This verse teaches, by implication, that there is a sense in which God *leads* us into temptation even as Satan *allures* us into the very same temptation. To say that God leads us into temptation is to use the word in its positive connotation. It is to say that God leads us into times of testing in order to strengthen and mature us. To say that Satan allures us into temptation is to use the word in its negative connotation. It is to say that Satan allures us into difficult testing in an effort to cripple and destroy us.

The fact that God leads and Satan allures into temptation is best illustrated in the life of Jesus himself. It was on the occasion of Jesus' baptism at the hands of John the Baptist that the Spirit of God descended upon Him and the voice of God communicated the divine favor to Him. (See Matthew 3:16-17.) At once, the Holy Spirit drove Jesus into the desert "to be tempted by the devil" (4:1b). Clearly, God *led* Jesus into temptation insofar as He drove Jesus into the wilderness for the express purpose of being tempted by the devil. By the same token, Satan attempted to *allure* Jesus into a position of weakness and vulnerability to the power of temptation as Satan was the actual agent tempting Jesus. God's purpose in leading Jesus into this time and place of testing was to prepare Jesus for the reception of the anointing which He would need to minister. Satan's purpose in alluring Jesus into temptation was to turn Jesus away from His loyalty to God His Father and so to eradicate the very possibility of ministering in the power of the kingdom of God. Of course, Jesus passed the test. We read of the aftermath of Jesus' wilderness temptations that He "returned to Galilee in the power of the Spirit . . ." (Luke 4:14a).

Some may feel that God leading and Satan alluring into temptation is unique to Jesus. Their thought is that God had to put Jesus to the test since He would have to say no to temptation and to sin in order to be the pure and perfect Lamb of God who would be fit to redeem humanity from sin. Since no other human being would need to fill the shoes of Jesus as a redeemer, it would not be necessary for God Himself to lead any other person into a desert of temptation. However, this perspective on temptation is not consistent with the biblical record. It is not only Jesus but all of God's people who are led by God and allured by Satan onto the testing ground of temptation. Let's look at one classic example from the Scriptures.

Consider Job. In God's eyes, he was a man of impeccable character. God described him as "blameless and upright, a man who fears God and shuns evil" (Job 1:8). In Satan's eyes, Job was a man of questionable motives. Satan portrayed him before God as one who served the Lord only in return for the blessings of a large family, great wealth, and divine protection upon his entire estate (1:9,10). In order to prove the integrity of Job, God permitted Satan to attack him through a series of catastrophes that robbed him of his children, much of his estate and his health (1:12-19; 2:6-8). Now, we might say that God *led* Job into temptation in order to prove his integrity. Satan attempted to *allure* Job away from his fidelity to God so that Job would "curse God and die" (2:9). God aimed at Job's vindication; Satan aimed at Job's destruction. In the end, God's purpose prevailed, and Job received a double portion of God's blessing (42:10).

When we are tempted, we need to be able to understand our trial both from God's perspective and from Satan's vantage point. God has led us to the temptation in order to "try" or "test" our faith with a view to our spiritual growth and maturity. Simultaneously, Satan allures us into the temptation to cripple our faith and to seduce us into enslavement to sin in order that he might ultimately destroy us. We must view every test of our faith from both angles if we are to properly understand temptation.

Unless we learn to view the difficult tests of life from both God's perspective and Satan's vantage point, we can be blown away by the seeming futility and unfairness of life's trials. I have had to learn this lesson in the past three years in what has seemed to me to be the most tragic of circumstances.

When I graduated from seminary in the Spring of 1988, I had two characteristics common to most young people as they venture into their careers. I was ambitious and I lived under the illusion of invincibility. While working for fourteen months at a local C.P.A. office to pay off some educational debt, I was chomping at the bits to start a church and prove myself successful in the ministry to which God had called me. However, before I was to establish a church, tragedy struck that was to put a seemingly unbearable damper on my zeal and shatter the illusion of invincibility under which I lived. In January of 1989, my father unexpectedly and suddenly died on his first week of retirement.

I had never been close to anyone who had died. The only funeral I had ever attended to my recollection was that of an uncle whom I did not remember meeting. Consequently, I had never felt the reality of human mortality. Two months after my father's death, I developed a nervous condition that made me suspect heart trouble. Medical tests revealed a normal, strong heart and excellent blood cholesterol level. I was diagnosed as being susceptible to anxiety attacks. My nervous condition was effectively treatable through mild tranquilizers. The upshot of this whole ordeal is that I was, through my father's death, becoming suddenly and staggeringly aware of my own mortality.

Approximately a year after the onset of nervous problems, I felt that I had, with God's help, reached a plateau of emotional stability sufficient to go ahead with my plans to start a church. With God's direction, I began The Sheepfold of Suffolk on April 15, 1990—Easter Sunday. While anxiety attacks recurred from time to time, I fought them in faith and became virtually independent of all nerve medication. My youthful ambition still had not adequately returned to be as excited and energetic about the ministry as I would have liked. Nonetheless, I continued to plug away at the ministry and God's blessing was evident for our first year. My nerves improved to the extent that I felt I had totally recovered. However, a couple of months into our second year of ministry tragedy struck again. In June of 1991, my mother had a slight heart attack. One week later, her heart failed and she died. She had lived to see me through my first year of pastoral ministry.

The loss of my parents at this time in my life has been a staggering trial of my faith. I am thirty-one, still single and just beginning my vocation. In some ways, I feel that I have had the rug pulled out from under me at just the time when I was due to start walking on my own. Even in those times when God's blessing was evident upon my ministry in the manifestation of his power and glory, feelings of despair and of futility seemed to be lurking just around the corner. My own sense of mortality distorted my views of God as my loving heavenly Father, magnified my imperfections in my own eyes and caused me to entertain feelings of guilt and of condemnation. If I needed anything at the time, it was to understand these difficult tests by seeing them both from God's perspective and from Satan's vantage point.

Through the eye of faith, I was able to see these difficult tests from God's vantage point. During my last academic quarter in seminary, I had followed a divine leading to pursue a hospital chaplaincy internship with the University of Southern California Medical Center little knowing that the focus of the internship would be on ministry to the dying and the bereaved. God was seeking to prepare me for my own time of bereavement. Secondly, God has given me reassurance of His goodness and mercy through this difficult time of my life. Let me relate to you just how He did this.

After my father's death and before establishing The Sheepfold, I was driving one Sunday morning to the church of which I was a member in Virginia Beach, Virginia. My body was ill from shot nerves and my mind was plagued with condemning thoughts. Knowing that my present mindset made me unable to hear clearly from the Lord, I prayed in earnest asking God to please have someone give me a word from him that morning. I specified that it did not have to be a public word in front of the whole church. I would be just as happy if it were a word delivered in private.

Arriving at church, I picked a chair and saved my seat with my Bible while I went off to the prayer room. When I returned to my seat, there was a slip of paper in it with the words "Jeremiah 29:11" written on it. Looking this verse up in my Bible, I found these reassuring words: "`For I know the plans I have for you,' declares the Lord, `plans to prosper you and not to harm you, plans to give you hope and a future'."

God's perspective on the trial of my faith that resulted from my parents' death is evident from this instance of personal reassurance. My mortality is not something to be afraid of. God is my loving heavenly Father who prospers me and does not harm me. He has a plan for my life and He will bring it to pass. What better way to grow in grace and in faith than to hold onto this assurance in the face of such great loss and bereavement?

In the process of gaining God's perspective on such trials of my faith, I have come the more easily to see them from Satan's vantage point as well. Satan tries to make death look ultimate and life look futile. Thus he tries to deprive us of the joy and peace imparted through God's promises to give His children abundant life in this world and an eternal life of felicity in the world to come. It is Satan who planted the thoughts of condemnation and fear in my mind in an effort to distort in my thinking the biblical depiction of God as my loving heavenly Father.

Seeing my trials from both God's perspective and Satan's vantage point has enabled me to joyfully embrace God's overtures of love and firmly resist Satan's lies of condemnation. It has helped me to overcome feelings of despair and futility. I believe it has made me much more adequate to counsel others who face similar circumstances in their lives as well.

I have taken an extreme example to illustrate the need for all God's people to view every trial from the perspectives of both God and Satan. Unless we are able to see God's good purpose always winning out over Satan's malevolent purpose, we are likely to face difficult trials with a feeling of futility and hopelessness. But when we see with the eye of faith the sovereign hand of God working our greater good through every plot of Satan against us, we will find every test a stepping-stone to growth. Thus

God grants us kingdom protection from the pitfalls of temptation by enabling us to understand temptation.

Facing Temptation

We must understand temptation precisely because we will inevitably *face* it. The second way in which God grants us kingdom protection from the ill-effects of temptation and from the ill-will of the tempter is by enabling us to face temptation. And how will we fare when we face temptation? It all depends upon how we choose to respond.

Just as temptation itself involves an *external* conflict between God's purpose to develop us and Satan's purpose to destroy us, so our facing temptation involves an *internal* conflict between the desire of our new nature to serve God and the pull of our old nature to serve Satan. Therefore, to face temptation squarely and honestly is to pause at a fork in the road of our lives and to make a deliberate decision about which way we will go. For each temptation poses the same challenge: "Choose . . . this day whom you will serve" (Joshua 24:15). Our choices in the face of temptation will chart the course of our lives for good or evil. Much wisdom is in the anonymous saying, "Sow a thought, reap an act; sow an act, reap a habit; sow a habit, reap a lifestyle; sow a lifestyle, reap a destiny."

Since our responses to temptation are of the utmost importance in determining the course of our lives for good or evil, the Bible gives us careful instruction about how we *should not* respond to temptation and about how we *should* respond. We will focus first on the warning of Scripture and then on the instruction of Scripture in the matter of facing temptation.

What is the warning of Scripture in the matter of facing temptation? It is summed up in the word that God spoke to the people of Israel: "Ye shall not tempt the Lord your God, as ye tempted him in Massah" (Deuteronomy 6:16). We have in this verse a warning that is given in both precept and example. The precept simply states that humankind is not to tempt God. That is, we are not to "try" or "test" God to see if God is reliable and trustworthy. We are simply to trust and obey God. To make sure we understand this point, God gives us an illustration of what it means to tempt Him in the way the children of Israel behaved at Massah. What happened there? Let's briefly review a portion of Israel's history leading up to Massah in order to understand the significance of what happened.

The children of Israel witnessed many miracles of protection and provision that God performed on their behalf as He delivered them out of Egyptian bondage and guided them through their wilderness wanderings. They saw the plagues with which their God devastated Egypt in order to deliver His people out of the hands of their oppressive taskmasters. They saw the supernatural opening of the Red Sea as God protected them from Pharaoh's army and provided them safe passageway through the Sea. They observed the miraculous purification of the bitter waters of Marah through which God provided for the thirst of His people in the wilderness. They gratefully partook of the manna and quail that God rained down upon the desert floor in the Desert of Sin in order to sustain and nourish them there. By this point the Israelites should have been so impressed with God's track record in caring for them that they would trust God in every circumstance—or so you would think.

The next stop was Massah. There the Israelites found no water to drink. (See Exodus 17:1.) Now, the appropriate response to the situation would have been for the people to look to God to provide them with water. But they did not respond this way at all. We read that the people quarreled with Moses. They said to him, "Give us water to drink" (17:2). They also tested God. They asked this very revealing question: "Is the Lord among us or not?" (17:7). The biblical account says that this response put God to the test (17:7). Despite all His goodness to them on previous occasions, the children of Israel put God on trial to see if He would prove faithful in meeting their present need. Rather than submitting to this hardship as a test of their faith in God, they turned it into a test of God's faithfulness to them.

When we face temptation, we must heed the warning of Scripture not to put God to the test. That is, we must be careful that we trust God through every hardship of life and not become bitter against Him and question His faithfulness to us. We may not bluntly verbalize the question, "Is God among us or not?" But we can sometimes pose this question through our attitudes and actions in times of trial. This is what our lives say when we allow the pressures of life to move us to anxiety or self-pity.

I once heard a dear Christian sister relate a personal experience that graphically illustrates the point. She was out driving one day when the pressures of life began to close in upon her mind. When she got to her destination, she had emotionally reached a breaking point. She parked her car and then—in anger and self-pity—began to cry and pound her fists against the steering wheel. As she was sobbing, the Lord spoke clearly to her spirit and said, "You're wasting everything I've done for you." What was God saying? He was saying, "Why are you putting Me to the test? I've already given you everything you need to be an overcomer in every circumstance of life. Why don't you trust Me and rest in My grace? Why don't you cast your cares upon Me and receive My peace?

Trusting God's wisdom and benevolence toward us will enable us to face the trials of life as God desires. Rather than putting God to the test by questioning His faithfulness to us, our trust of God will enable us to rest in His grace and enjoy His peace.

We have considered the warning of Scripture that teaches us how *not* to respond to temptation. We are not to put God to the test. We turn now to consider the instruction of Scripture that teaches us how *to* respond to the testing of our faith. And how does the Scripture instruct us in this matter? It exhorts us to see our trials from God's vantage point and rejoice in the face of every trial.

If we are to respond appropriately to temptation, we must see temptation as God sees it. We must acknowledge three facts about our trials.

First, God only leads us into times of testing to strengthen and mature us. The Bible says, " . . . the testing of our faith develops perseverance. Perseverance must finish its work so that you will be mature and complete, not lacking anything" (James 1:3,4). We must determine not to despair because of the severity of our trials. Rather, we must determine to focus upon the positive purpose that the trial is meant to serve.

Second, God has not been partial in leading us into the particular kind of test that we are facing. Others have faced the very same temptations we encounter. The Bible says, "No temptation has seized you except what is common to man" (1 Corinthians 10:13a). We must determine not to become bitter and complain, "Why me, Lord?" Rather than complaining that our trials are unjust, we must decide to implicitly trust God's wisdom and benevolence in permitting us to face the hardships that come our way.

Third, God restrains the power of temptation so that it cannot overcome us. The Bible says that God " . . . will not let you be tempted beyond what you can bear. But when you are tempted, he will also provide a way out so that you can stand up under it" (1 Corinthians 10:13b). We must resist the tendency to become fearful that we will break under the pressure. Rather, we must firmly decide to confidently endure every test while casting all anxiety upon the Lord. (See 1 Peter 5:7.)

To see our temptations from God's perspective is to see in each trial of our faith God's purpose in bringing it, God's impartiality in allowing it *in our lives* and God's power in restraining it. When we thus have God's perspective on temptation as the trying of our faith, we will be able to respond as God would have us to by facing each test with a spirit of rejoicing. We will be enabled to heed the exhortation of James: "Consider it pure joy, my brothers, whenever you face trials of many kinds" (1:2). And why are we to rejoice when tested? We are to do so because rejoicing in our times of trial breaks the power of temptation for evil and enhances its power for good.

Merlin Carothers tells of a young woman who learned firsthand that rejoicing in the face of hardship could effectively turn trying circumstances around for her good.(4)

This young woman had been embarrassed by circumstances in her personal life to the point that she lost her self-respect. To cope with feelings of insecurity, she became gluttonous. As she rapidly gained weight, her husband lost interest in her and became attracted to other women. Eventually, he moved out and filed for a divorce.

With her husband gone and bills piling up, this woman became a nervous wreck. While she faithfully attended church, read her Bible and received much encouragement from friends, she became depressed to the point of considering suicide. But then she was given a copy of Merlin Carothers' book, *Prison To Praise.* In reading this book, she was impressed to learn how her life could be changed by giving thanks to God for *every* circumstance of life—even those circumstances of life that seem to have no redeeming value.

She turned to the Lord in prayer:

> God, I thank You that my life is just as it is. Every problem I have has been Your gift to bring me to the place where I am right now. You wouldn't have permitted any of these things to happen if You hadn't known that it was best for me. God, You really *do* love me! I mean it God, I *know* You do love me.

As she was praying, the dog started barking as the mailman had come to her door. She started to launch into her usual tirade against the dog for barking when she remembered that she was supposed to be thankful for everything. So, she asked God to forgive her and thanked Him for her barking dog.

Opening the door, she greeted the mailman who delivered a letter from her husband. In it, he said that he believed the two of them could work things out to redeem their marriage if she were willing. Excited by God's timely response to her prayer, she was restored in her self-esteem and immediately began a weight loss program. Her self-esteem and her marriage were restored. In a short time, she was down to a much more ideal weight. All of her friends complimented her on how good she looked. This young woman had faced a difficult trial that had much potential for evil. She had even been driven to thoughts of suicide. But by learning to rejoice in the face of her trial, she was affirming her faith in the wisdom and benevolence of God. The result was that her trials were turned around for her good.

As we learn to rejoice in our trials, we too will experience God's purpose to make the hardships of our lives serve our ultimate good. By thus seeing our hardships as God sees them and rejoicing in the midst of them, we learn how to appropriately face temptation.

Enduring Temptation

The third way in which God grants us kingdom protection against the ill-effects of temptation and the ill-will of the tempter is by enabling us to *endure* temptation. And how does God enable us to endure temptation? He does so by imparting to us an understanding of the work of our *adversary* against us and that of our *advocate* for us. If we are to endure temptation, we must know both our adversary and our advocate.

First of all, we must know our adversary if we are to endure temptation. The Bible teaches that our lives are the battleground upon which spiritual warfare is being waged between God and Satan. God fights for our liberation and salvation. Satan fights for our bondage and destruction. God brings hardships in our lives to strengthen and mature us. Satan brings hardships in our lives to weaken and cripple us. Applying this perspective of spiritual warfare to our trials enlightens us to the fact that we have an invisible adversary of whom we must be wary. We must be wary of his use of subtlety and deception to cause us to justify sin and to fall into temptation with little or no conscience in the matter. The Apostle Peter wrote, "Be self-controlled and alert. Your enemy the devil prowls around like a roaring lion looking for someone to devour" (1 Peter 5:8). To know that we have an invisible adversary and to be on the alert against his subtlety and deception is the first step toward enduring temptation.

Many Christians are weakened in their ability to endure temptation because of their denial of the existence of the adversary. Denial of the existence of the devil and his demons leads to ignorance of Satan's devices by which he deceives and destroys. Unfortunately, this spiritual blindness is reinforced by many liberal Bible scholars and professors through their proposal of a so-called "accommodation theory."(5) This theory maintains that Jesus Himself was too spiritually enlightened to believe in the devil and his demons. But Jesus lived in a primitive society in which people not only believed in such evil powers but maintained that these powers caused all of the ills of the world, including physical sickness. According to this theory, Jesus had a heart for these primitive people and wanted to heal them without offending them. Therefore, He cast out devils that he didn't believe in! The ignorant people, not knowing any difference, believed that the evil spirits came out. Therefore, they manifested healing in their bodies of what were probably no more than psychosomatic conditions to start with. I concur with Maxwell Whyte's conclusion: "Anyone who believes the Bible to be the Word of God cannot possibly accept this theory."(6)

It has been said that a man with an experience is never at the mercy of a man with an argument. Permit me to say that I *believe* in the existence of the devil and his demons because God's Word clearly teaches their reality. But I *know* firsthand of their existence through my own past experience of demonization and demonic harassment. In the interest of helping the reader take seriously the admonition of Scripture to be alert to the devil's workings and knowledgeable of his devices (see 1 Peter 5:8 and 2 Corinthians 2:11), I will essay here my experience of the reality of the demonic realm and my deliverance from the power of the same.

My first encounter with the power and malevolence of the demonic realm came in my early childhood. I was approximately four years old when I began to have a recurring nightmare. In this nightmare, I saw a huge, complex machine with a long conveyor belt. As I observed this machine, a powerful force pulled me into it. I was then pulled along on the conveyor belt while various parts of this contraption were crushing and mangling my body, thus causing a great deal of mental and emotional turmoil. When at long last I was emitted from the machine, I took a sigh of relief only to be pulled back in and the process repeated.

This nightmare eventually became a vision that happened uexpectantly at any given time of the day. On one such occasion, my father, brother, and I were at my grandmother's house. Just before leaving, we were all standing in her den. My father and grandmother were standing on opposite sides of her pot-belly stove exchanging final words while my brother Mason and I were standing on opposite sides of the doorway. Without a moment's notice, my consciousness was totally subdued and I was pulled into the vision again. I had no awareness of the real world — only of this tormenting machine. The intense torment caused me to burst into tears. Instantly, I snapped back to reality with three sets of startled eyes upon me. Simultaneously, my grandmother and father asked, "What's wrong with you?" Feeling ashamed to tell them the truth, I blurted out, "Mason hit me!" Of course, they all knew that wasn't so.

Some time later, my mother took me for several consecutive nights to a revival held in a Church of God. Each night, I behaved until the preaching started. But when the minister began to preach, I became tormented again and began to cry. Finally, the evangelist discerned that the problem was demonic and called for my mother to bring me forward. He prayed over me and said that he felt seven evil spirits leave my body one by one. For the rest of that service and the rest of the revival, I was at peace. I have not had a recurrence of this tormenting vision since.

While many might be inclined to say that such experiences are entirely subjective and can be understood purely on a psychological level, my next encounter with the demonic left in its wake tangible evidence that cannot be explained in psychological terms. Interestingly enough, this encounter came shortly after my conversion to Christ at age ten.

On the evening of the encounter, my brother and I (who shared the same bedroom) had already turned the lights out and gone to bed. Not being sleepy, I became restless. I decided to sit up in bed for awhile. Suddenly, I thought I saw a dark form about the size of a bear come into the room and walk toward my brother's bed. As I strained my eyes to see it, I was convinced at one moment that it was actually there and at the next moment that I was merely imagining it.

As the bear-like figure disappeared from sight, I began to see just a few inches in front of my eyes a cartoon-like hornet whose body was lit up and whose wings were buzzing. I believe now that the hornet was sent to divert my attention from the bear-like figure that was sent to harm my brother in some way. As I curiously watched the hornet, I felt the bed getting shorter under me so that my head and feet hung over the bed. Needless to say, I was disturbed. However, I felt relieved when I noticed that there stood between my bed and the wall a man dressed in what appeared to be a Roman suit of armor. I was relieved because I figured he was standing there to protect me from any harm.

Suddenly, the scene changed, and I was at my cousin's house several miles away. Judging from the appearance of the room, I knew that I was lying on his couch in the living room. But the couch felt as if it were a comfortable, king-sized bed. As I lay there, I looked up at the lintel of the bathroom doorway. From the lintel hung several strings. From the strings hung different types of insects whose bodies were dangling and casting light as if from the facets of a diamond.

The vision had gone much too far for my comfort, so I yelled, "Mama!" In response, I heard an eerie, demonic voice respond slowly and with a drawl, "What matters?" Fear paralyzed me for a couple of minutes. Finally, I summoned enough courage to cry out again, "Mama!" This time, I heard my mother's footsteps coming toward the room. As soon as she walked into the room and turned the lights on, the vision changed and I was back to my own room again.

Everything I've related in this second encounter so far could be explained away by the skeptic. But, tangible evidence indicated that something had happened in the room. First, my body was turned sideways on the bed with my head hanging from one side of the bed and my feet from the other. Second, my brother—who slept through the whole thing—had been turned completely around in his bed. His head was at the foot end of the bed and his feet were on the pillow! This had never happened to him before. When my mother awakened him and asked how he got turned around, he had no explanation.

The meaning of this event puzzled me for some time. My brother and I had both been saved a fairly short time when it took place. The demonic powers that manifested themselves in our room that night were undoubtedly intent upon more than turning us around in our beds. Satan intended to put us to sleep spiritually and turn us away from the Lord.

I believe that God permitted me to be awake through this whole encounter so that I would, in years to come, be aware of Satan's devices by which to turn my brother and me away from the Lord. Such awareness would enable me to pray for kingdom protection for both of us to preserve us from the deceptive and destructive plots of the evil one. For our purposes here, however, I relate these personal experiences to impress upon the reader both the reality of the adversary and the need to be on the alert to his devices against us.

When we know our adversary, we can resist his every attempt to deceive and destroy us. The devil plays upon our vulnerabilities by alluring us with enchanting pictures of the things our fallen natures desire. He parades before us in deceptive beauty things that appeal to "the cravings of sinful man, the lust of his eyes, and the boasting of what he has and does" (1 John 2:16). He intends to convince us that so-called "sinful pleasures" are not sinful at all. If he is successful in his *deceptive* schemes, he will be successful in causing us to fall into temptation. If we do fall, we become prey to his *destructive* schemes against us.

When Jesus taught us to pray, "And lead us not into temptation, but deliver us from the evil one" (Matthew 6:13), He gave a plea for kingdom protection against the ill-effects of temptation and the ill-will of the tempter. This prayer is answered, first of all, through divine illumination to the reality, the malevolence and the deceptive and destructive schemes of the evil one. If we are to endure temptation, we must know our adversary.

Second, we must know our *advocate* if we are to endure temptation. An advocate is the equivalent of a defense attorney. He speaks before a court of law in behalf of one who is under accusation. We read of the adversary of the saints that he "accuses them before God day and night" (Revelation 12:10). Never do we fall into temptation and sin but that Satan appears before the throne of the Judge of all the earth to prosecute us and call for a swift sentence. But we need not fear the accusations of the adversary because our advocate is always there to speak in our defense. The Apostle John wrote, "And if any man sin, we have an advocate with the Father, Jesus Christ the righteous: and he is the propitiation for our sins: and not for ours only, but also for the sins of the whole world" (1 John 2:1, 2). Jesus ever represents us before God's throne by pleading His blood as the payment for our sins by which we are forgiven of all sins—past, present, and future—and welcomed into God's favor.

How does knowing our advocate enable us to endure temptation? It does so in two ways. It imparts to us in the face of our temptations divine encouragement and divine empowerment.

Knowing our advocate *encourages* us to endure temptation. One of the things that makes our trials so cumbersome is having to endure them alone. Sometimes people try to sympathize with us when they have never faced the difficult circumstances we face. But because they have not been in our situation, their sympathy has a hollow ring to it. It does not encourage us. Conversely, our advocate can always genuinely sympathize with us and encourage us in our times of temptation. Scripture says of Christ, "For we do not have a high priest who is unable to sympathize with our weaknesses, but we have one who has been tempted in every way, just as we are—yet was without sin" (Hebrews 4:15). The same author penned these words concerning our advocate: "Because he himself suffered when he was tempted, he is able to help those who are being tempted" (Hebrews 2:18). When we know Jesus as one who has faced and overcome every temptation that comes our way and who is available to help us respond appropriately in our times of trial, we are encouraged to fight the good fight of faith. Truly, knowing our advocate *encourages* us to faithfully endure every temptation.

Knowing our advocate also *empowers* us to endure temptation. Jesus' role as our advocate is synonymous with that of our high priest. As our high priest, He intercedes for us continually before God. That is, He always prays for us. All of His prayers petition for our complete salvation from everything that would endanger or harm us. Jesus prays that God our Father will empower and enable us to endure temptation. Because our high priest so intercedes for us, we can pray with confidence for God's sustaining grace to see us through. This is the point of the writer of Hebrews who, having discussed the faithful intercession of our high priest, encourages us with these words: "Let us then approach the throne of grace with confidence, so that we may receive mercy and find grace to help us in our time of need" (4:16). When we pray for God's grace to respond to temptation as we should, He answers the prayer by strengthening us to endure every trial. Truly, knowing our advocate *empowers* us to endure temptation.

Knowing our advocate is more than knowing about Him. It is knowing Him with the knowledge of personal, intimate relationship. Without such knowledge, it is easy to have a mistaken image of the advocate that would make Him out to be more of an adversary. For example, many people who fail to understand Jesus' role as their advocate imagine God as a heavy-handed dictator just waiting for them to get out of line so that He can punish them. They view every unpleasant and tragic circumstance that comes their way as punishment from God for their imperfections. Even the tests that God brings into their lives to strengthen and mature them are perceived as the bitter cup of God's wrath. Such a view of God fails to consider that God through Christ has graciously forgiven our sins and has just as freely received us into His favor. Such a view of God is alien to the one that Christ imparts—that of a loving heavenly Father who delights in blessing and protecting His children.

To know our advocate is to know Jesus as Savior. It is to know that He took our place in death and that His blood avails for our sins. It is to know that His righteousness has been freely credited to our account so that God would no more condemn us than He would condemn Jesus. When we know our advocate, we don't face life's trials with a paralyzing fear of God's wrath and condemnation. We are no longer children of wrath with condemnation hanging over our heads. Now, we can face life's trials as stepping-stones to growth in Christian character. Knowing Jesus as our advocate in heaven who defends us before the throne of the Judge of all the earth encourages and empowers us to endure temptation.

Overcoming Temptation

The final way in which God grants us kingdom protection from the ill-effects of temptation and from the ill-will of the tempter is by enabling us to *overcome* temptation. While temptation is a fact of life, it is not meant to be our natural element. Just as the children of Israel were not intended by God to wander around in the wilderness of temptation endlessly but to pass through the desert and into the Promised Land, so we are not meant to wander around in the wilderness of temptation but to pass through this wasteland into God's greater blessing. God enables us to understand, face and endure temptation in order that we might overcome it and reap the reward for passing the test. As the apostle James wrote, "Blessed is the man who perseveres under trial, because when he has stood the test, he will receive the crown of life that God has promised to those who love him" (1:12).

How does God enable us to overcome temptation? Jesus answered this question for us in the words of our text. We are to pray, "Lead us not into temptation, but deliver us from the evil one" (Matthew 6:13). Jesus taught us to pray this petition precisely because prayer is the key to overcoming temptation.

Now we have already seen that this petition of prayer that is before us teaches, by implication, that God leads us into temptation for a constructive purpose even as Satan allures us into the very same temptation for a destructive purpose. We have seen that God will not spare us temptation even though He limits the severity of the temptation so that it will not be too great for us to bear. Since temptation is within God's will and is inescapable, we might be inclined to wonder what the point would be in praying at all for deliverance from temptation and from the evil one.

Let me respond to this curiosity by suggesting that the petition of the Lord's Prayer that is before us teaches, again by implication, that *the degree* to which we are subjected to temptation is limited by our prayers for God's gracious deliverance. While God will not allow the righteous to be tempted beyond what they are able to bear (see 1 Corinthians 10:13), He also hears their cry for help and delivers them. (See Psalm 34:15,17.) God welcomes our humble plea for deliverance from hard testings that would make us inclined to succumb to the evil one. Such a plea expresses both our loyalty to God and the awareness of our dependence upon Him.

Now we can learn an important lesson from this petition by inverting it. If we are to pray for deliverance from overbearing temptations and from the malevolence of the tempter, such prayer must be necessary to overcoming temptation. Conversely, if we do *not* pray for such deliverance, *we cannot overcome temptation.* Without prayerful dependence upon God in our times of difficult testing, we will surely fail. Let's examine a couple of examples from the gospels that emphasize the importance of prayer in overcoming temptation.

Luke tells us that at the Last Supper Jesus talked to His disciples about finding greatness through service and not through self-exaltation. Right in the middle of this discourse, Jesus turned to Peter and said, "Simon, Simon, Satan has asked to sift you as wheat. But I have prayed for you, Simon, that your faith may not fail. And when you have turned back, strengthen your brothers" (Luke 22:31, 32). Peter objected, "Lord, I am ready to go with you to prison and to death" (vs. 33). Jesus' response was prophetic: "I tell you, Peter, before the rooster crows today, you will deny three times that you know me" (vs. 34). End of conversation.

Now let's analyze this brief interchange between Jesus and Peter. Jesus learned by divine means that Satan had petitioned God for permission to tempt Peter and that God had granted the permission requested. And how did Jesus respond to this revelation? We might have expected Him to respond by giving Peter advance warning of the attack and a detailed strategy for outwitting the devil and overcoming his temptation. But Jesus did not seek to prepare Peter for the fiery trials of the devil in this way. He simply said to Peter, "I am praying for you so that your faith will remain strong." When Peter replied by proudly asserting his loyalty to Christ even to the point of death, Jesus did not use Peter's profession of loyalty as the basis for a pep talk motivating Peter to courageously stand the test. On the contrary, Jesus foretold Peter's failure and his conversion and gave instruction concerning Peter's role in encouraging the other disciples when the same tests would shake their faith. Not being ignorant of Peter's weakness or his imminent fall, Jesus expected His prayer to be answered to the end that Peter would be delivered from the grasp of the evil one. Clearly, Jesus' prayer for Peter was the means by which Peter was delivered from the malevolence of the tempter.

In Peter's case, Jesus' prayer enabled him to ultimately overcome temptation. Shortly afterward, Jesus taught His disciples the value of their *own* prayers in overcoming temptation. Luke tells us that Jesus went with his disciples to the Mount of Olives to pray just before his arrest. Arriving at the place of prayer, Jesus said to the disciples,

"Pray that you will not fall into temptation" (Luke 22:40). Then Jesus went some distance beyond them to pray alone. He prayed for the strength to submit to God's will in enduring His own imminent suffering. Returning to the disciples, He found them asleep. Awakening them, He said, "Get up and pray so that you will not fall into temptation" (vs. 46).

On this occasion, Jesus did not tell His disciples to recite to one another the convincing proofs of His messiahship in order to strengthen their faith. He did not appeal to their loyalty to Him as the grounds for willingly giving their lives for the faith in order that their righteous blood might be the seed of the Church. On the contrary, He simply told them to pray that they would be spared from temptation. As far as Jesus was concerned, the disciples' prayers for themselves, not simply His prayers for them, were to be the means by which they would overcome temptation.

Prayer is also the key by which we overcome temptation. The prayers of Jesus for us certainly serve an important purpose in preserving us from the dangers of succumbing to temptation. We've already seen that Jesus *defends* us before God as our advocate by *interceding* for us as our high priest. Jesus is praying for us. But his prayers alone are not the only means that bring us kingdom protection in the face of temptation. Our prayers for ourselves are also a necessary means to the same protection. This is why it is essential that we pray, "Lead us not into temptation, but deliver us from the evil one" (Matthew 6:13).

Remembering that we are addressing our Father in heaven will help us to understand the significance of this petition of the Lord's Prayer. We are petitioning our heavenly Father to be merciful to us and help us in our times of testing. In order to gain a better understanding of the import of this petition, allow me to illustrate how it is analogous to the petition that a son might make to his earthly parents.

Imagine earthly parents who are rearing a son. They take delight in the playfulness and happiness of their son's childhood. But as the boy gets old enough to assume some responsibility in helping his parents, they give him chores to do around the house and in the yard. They are intent upon teaching him to be hard-working and industrious so that he will grow up highly motivated to be responsible and to be an achiever.

Now imagine that the parents, in their zeal, overdo it and give their son more responsibility than his age and personal development merits. One day, the boy starts to cry. When the parents ask what's wrong, he says, "I want to please you and do my chores, but there's just so much that I have to do that I hardly have time to have fun anymore. I don't get to spend much time with my friends anymore. Do I have to do all of this?" What does this plea tell the parents? It tells them that too much responsibility for their young son has turned the joy of labor into the drudgery of labor. This is hardly the way to motivate him to be a high achiever in life. Therefore, they will lighten his load until he is old enough and mature enough to handle more responsibility without feeling overburdened by it.

Now, the Bible says, "As a father has compassion on his children, so the Lord has compassion on those who fear him; for he knows how we are formed, he remembers that we are dust" (Psalm 103:13, 14). God knows our weaknesses and vulnerabilities. He does not allow tests to come into our lives to destroy us. He allows us to be tested at our weak points in order to strengthen and mature us so that we may be conformed to his image. One of the signs that the tests are doing their job is that they do not lead us to rebel against God in anger but to plead with him in humility for help.

When God hears our cry for help, He compassionately comes to our aid so that we won't be overburdened by our tests. This cry for help is expressed in the plea, "Lead us not into temptation, but deliver us from the evil one" (Matthew 6:13). Such prayer is the key to overcoming temptation.

Summing It Up

Temptation is a fact of life. God does not grant us immunity to temptation but does grant us kingdom protection from the ill-effects of temptation and from the ill-will of our malevolent tempter. He does so by enabling us to understand, face, endure and overcome temptation.

First of all, God enables us to understand temptation. The Bible teaches us that temptation must be viewed from the perspectives of God and Satan. God leads us into temptations to test us with a view to strengthening us and bringing us to greater Christian maturity. Satan allures us into the very same temptations in order to weaken us, cripple our faith and destroy us. When we understand temptation correctly, we can learn to submit to God's purposes in every test and benefit by doing so.

Second, God enables us to face temptation. He does so by teaching us how *not* to respond to temptation and how *to* respond. We are not to respond by putting God to the test. That is, we are not to question God's goodness and faithfulness to us when we are tempted. The proper response is to trust that God has a worthy purpose in allowing the test to come our way and to submit to the test in a spirit of rejoicing.

Third, God enables us to endure temptation. He does so by enlightening us to the devices of our adversary and the defenses of our advocate. Our adversary endeavors to deceive us in order that he might destroy us even as he accuses us before the Judge of all the earth. But our advocate defends us through appealing to His atoning blood shed for us and through interceding for us that we might be strengthened to endure. In knowing Jesus, our advocate, we are encouraged and enabled to endure temptation.

Finally, God enables us to overcome temptation. He does so by giving to us the key to the overcoming of temptation in the petition, "Lead us not into temptation, but deliver us from the evil one" (Matthew 6:13). In answer to this petition God our Father, moved by compassion toward His children, lifts the burden of temptation from our shoulders so that we will not be overcome by it.

Let's resolve in our hearts that we will prayerfully look to God for help in times of difficult trial. Furthermore, let's resolve in accordance with Jesus' outline for prayer that we will make this plea a part of our daily prayer regimen. As we do, we will learn that we do not have to face life's hardships and trials alone. For in answer to our prayers, God will grant us kingdom protection.

Notes

1. Charles Stanley, *Temptation* (Nashville: Thomas Nelson Publishers, 1988), p. 75.

2. Ibid., p. 33.

3. John Gage Allee, ed., *Webster's Encyclopedia of Dictionaries* (U.S.A.: Ottenheimer Publishers, Inc., 1958), p. 383.

4. Merlin R. Carothers, *Power In Praise*, Escondido, California: Merlin R. Carothers, 1972), pp. 7,8.

5. H. A. Maxwell Whyte, *Demons and Deliverance* (Springdale, Pennsylvania: Whitaker House, 1989), p. 88.

6. Ibid.

Chapter Eight

Kingdom Promotion

> *. . . for yours is the kingdom and the power and the glory forever. Amen.*—Matthew 6:13b (NIV footnote)

One of the greatest frustrations I have encountered in founding a local church is motivating people to praise God. I faithfully taught the handful of people who first came to the Sheepfold that our praises of God are ordained by Him to be the means for ushering His presence into the sanctuary. I emphasized the role of praise in so exalting God our King that Satan's forces are put to flight and his strongholds in our lives are demolished. I explained that through praise God's people come to know in their own experience the Spirit-filled life characterized by victorious Christian living. Yet, for all my encouragement to praise, I often found myself up front pouring out my praises to God while my ears told me that the rest of the congregation had comfortably assumed the role of silent spectators. I do not blame them. I was endeavoring to lead them into exuberant, wholehearted worship of God when most of them had no previous experience of such. I relate this matter of personal frustration to emphasize that a great deal of the church world fails to grasp the purpose and importance of praise.

In the closing doxology of the Lord's Prayer, Jesus taught us the purpose and importance of praise. Giving God the praise that is due Him promotes the kingdom of God and paralyzes the kingdom of Satan. In the prayer thus far, we have petitioned God for the meeting of our needs in order that God's kingdom be promoted. We have also petitioned God for deliverance from the malevolence of the tempter in order that Satan's kingdom be paralyzed. And on what grounds can we offer these petitions for the progress of God's kingdom and the regress of Satan's? The grounds for such petitions are revealed in the threefold doxology of praise with which the Lord's Prayer ends: "For yours is the kingdom and the power and the glory forever. Amen" (Matthew 6:13b; NIV footnote).

This chapter focuses on praise as it is depicted in the Lord's Prayer as a whole and in the closing doxology in particular. We will find that the Lord's Prayer teaches us two important lessons about praise. First, praise is the key to prayer. Second, praise is the key to the promotion of God's kingdom. Let's consider these lessons in order.

Praise: The Key To Prayer

First of all, praise is the key to prayer, for the praise of God invites the presence of God among us. When God is present among us, we are able to truly commune with Him through prayer.

What is the relationship between praise and prayer? This question is answered for us in the Lord's Prayer. In our Lord's inspired outline of prayer, we learn that praise:

1. envelops prayer
2. enables prayer
3. empowers prayer

First of all, praise envelops prayer. That is, praise both introduces and concludes prayer. How is this seen in our Lord's outline of prayer? The Lord's Prayer begins with the hallowing of God's name. We hold God in highest esteem by declaring that His name is separate from and superior to all other names. The Lord's Prayer ends with praise. We acknowledge God's sovereign and majestic rule over all as we ascribe to Him the kingdom, the power, and the glory. When we pray as Jesus taught us to pray, our prayers will be enveloped with praise.

Why is it important that our prayers be enveloped with praise? Because praise provides the appropriate focus for prayer. When our prayers are enveloped in praise, they are focused upon God and not upon ourselves. The result is that we honor God by putting His kingdom interests ahead of personal concerns. Thus prayers enveloped in praise truly promote God's kingdom.

The Bible gives a vivid example of how praise enveloping prayer promotes God's kingdom. (See Acts 16:11-34.) We read of the missionary work of Paul and Silas in the Macedonian capital of Philippi. For several days, a slave girl who was possessed with a spirit of divination followed them around and agitated them. Finally, Paul cast the demon out of this girl and incurred the wrath of the girl's owners. Now that she had lost her fortune-telling ability, they could no longer make money from her services. In revenge, they brought charges against Paul and Silas before the magistrates of the city and had them thrown in prison.

Locked away in the maximum security cell with their feet fastened in the stocks, Paul and Silas could have entertained feelings of anger at their unfair treatment. They could have become anxious and fearful at the uncertainty of their plight. Instead, they spent their time behind bars "praying and singing hymns to God" (vs. 25). Their prayers were not enveloped with anger, worry, or fear. Their prayers were enveloped with praise and had such an effect upon the atmosphere in that prison that the other prisoners forgot about themselves and became engrossed in the worship of Paul and Silas. The Bible says the prisoners were "listening to them" (vs. 25).

Because Paul and Silas praised and prayed and praised, God sent a violent earthquake that threw open the doors of the prison and caused the chains to fall from the hands of all of the prisoners. The praise-enveloped prayers of Paul and Silas promoted God's kingdom interests in that prison. We see this through two details. First, the chains fell from the hands of all the prisoners and yet none tried to escape. They must have all been converted! Second, as a result of the event, the jailer and his family were saved and baptized that night. God's kingdom was established in that prison as a result of praise-enveloped prayers.

When we face difficult circumstances, we are inclined to pray according to the emotions of the moment. Such praying is inevitably ineffective. God is not moved by emotions—He is moved by faith. To pray in faith, we must get our eyes off of ourselves and our circumstances and onto God. We do this as we learn to let our prayers be enshrined in praise. When praise envelops our prayers, our prayers will not be ineffective. To the contrary, they will move the hand of God on our behalf in such a way as to promote His kingdom.

Not only does praise envelop prayer, but praise also enables prayer. Praise brings us into communion with God. In communion with God we can pray with the assurance that our prayers are heard. Such assurance enables us to present our petitions in faith that the God who hears us grants our requests. This is undoubtedly why we are instructed in the Lord's Prayer to *commune* with God through hallowing His name *before* petitioning God for the meeting of our individual needs. This same principle is communicated by Jesus elsewhere: "If you remain in me and my words remain in you, ask whatever you wish, and it will be given you" (John 15:7).

By bringing us into communion with God, praise focuses our thoughts upon God's power and goodness with the result that we become steadfast in trusting Him. The consequence of this revelation of God's power and goodness is that our prayers are moved by faith for the answer and not by fear of the consequences of unanswered prayer.

Praise produces an atmosphere conducive to faith in which prayers are answered. Lack of praise produces an atmosphere conducive to fear of the consequences of unanswered prayer. We must understand that prayers motivated by fear are prayers that God cannot answer.

I once heard of a couple who had a mentally retarded son. One day the three of them were working in the garden when a terrible storm struck. The son began to run toward the house with his mother and father right behind him. As the wind became more violent and the prospect for reaching safe cover became bleak, the parents fell on their knees and began to pray in a panic. The boy had reached the door and was holding it open for his parents. When he saw that his parents were on their knees praying, this mentally slow young man yelled out, "Come on, y'all! Scared prayin' ain't to no end!"

Scared praying is for those who aren't praisers. They are more preoccupied with themselves and their problems than they are with God. But praying in faith is the prayer of the praiser. We see this in Paul's exhortation to the Philippians. He first told them to praise. He said, "Rejoice in the Lord always" (4:4). He then told them to cast fear aside. He said, "Do not be anxious about anything" (4:6). Finally, they were to offer their prayer petitions to God in a spirit of thanksgiving. He said, " . . . in everything, by prayer and petition, with thanksgiving, present your requests to God" (4:6). This is the prayer of the praiser. And what is its effect? Such prayer causes the mind and heart to be guarded by God's peace, which, "transcends all understanding" (4:7). What begins with praise ends with the peaceful assurance of God's care. Clearly praise enables prayer.

Just as praise envelops and enables prayer, it also empowers prayer. It is significant that the last petition of the Lord's Prayer begins with the conjunction "for." We read, " . . . *for* yours is the kingdom and the power and the glory forever. Amen" (vs. 13b, NIV footnote; author's italics). The point of the petition is this: we can pray with confidence for God to pardon our sins, provide for our needs, and protect us from the evil one because God is able to meet these needs of our lives, for to God alone belong the kingdom, the power, and the glory. His sovereignty cannot be effectively challenged. When we praise God by ascribing to Him the kingdom, the power, and the glory, we release His power to answer our prayers. Thus praise empowers prayer.

Many times we pray our troubles to God in a spirit of despair and then wonder why God doesn't answer our prayers and turn our hardships around for our good. Nothing will stop the spirit of praise and so weaken our prayers as thinking that the hardships of our lives prove that God has forsaken us. He has only chosen to use some of the hardships of our lives as a means to working an eternal good in us. We need to allow praise to empower our prayers by learning to incorporate praise and thanksgiving into our prayers—especially when we feel weighted down by the cares of life.

Merlin Carothers, in his book entitled *Power In Praise,* relates a wealth of personal ministry encounters in which God privileged him to show others how to let praise empower their prayers in the face of hardship. One illustration will be sufficient here to solidify the point.(1)

A couple heard Carothers speak on the subject of praising God in every circumstance of life. As they drove home, they discussed the implications of this teaching for their own lives. They had a daughter who had been committed to an insane asylum several months earlier. Doctors had diagnosed her as hopelessly insane. While they had faithfully prayed for their daughter, their prayers had been to no avail. Now they could see that the fruitlessness of their prayers could be directly attributed to the fact that their prayers for their daughter had reflected their sense of despair and, therefore, had lacked the empowerment of praise and thanksgiving.

Carothers' teaching left this couple somewhat perplexed. Were they to assume an attitude of praise and thanksgiving to God when praying for their suffering daughter? It just didn't make sense. Yet Carothers had related many convincing illustrations of individuals who had experienced great deliverance in their lives when they learned to praise and thank God in the face of such trying circumstances of life.

When the couple got home, they both decided to put their questions aside and submit to the teaching they had received. The husband and wife knelt together and worshipped God, thanking him for his goodness to them and to their daughter. They expressed their trust in God's benevolence to them and entrusted their daughter to God's care. As they prayed, they received assurance that they were, through worship and thanksgiving, truly entering into a new dimension of trusting God with the care of their daughter.

The very next day, the couple got a call from the hospital psychiatrist who informed them their daughter had just evidenced a remarkable change for the better, and suggested they come and visit her. Two weeks later, their daughter was totally recovered and released to go home.

About a year after this event, Carothers had just finished a meeting when a young man in the audience came to him and introduced himself as the girl's brother. He told Carothers that his sister was now married and expecting. He described her as "the happiest girl in the world."

We must learn to let our prayers reflect a spirit of praise and gratitude even in the most difficult circumstances. This pleases God. God's counsel to us in this matter comes through the Apostle Paul, who wrote, "Give thanks in all circumstances, for this is God's will for you in Christ Jesus" (1 Thessalonians 5:18). He could just as well have said to *praise* God in all circumstances. As we learn this lesson, we will find that praise empowers our prayers and produces results in answer to our prayers that will truly promote God's kingdom.

Praise: The Key To Kingdom Promotion

We have seen that praise is the key to prayer. Praise envelops, enables, and empowers prayer. Now, let's focus on praise as the key to kingdom promotion. Through praise, we promote God's kingdom in our lives and in our world.

This study has shown us that the theme of the Lord's Prayer is the kingdom of God. Now it is not without significance that a prayer whose theme is the kingdom of God would both begin and end with the praise of God. To praise God is to submit to His kingdom. It is to yield to God our King both our obedience and our service. By thus enabling us to submit to God's rule over us, praise promotes God's kingdom.

In order to see just how praise promotes God's kingdom, we will focus upon the closing doxology of the Lord's Prayer. Jesus taught us to pray, "For yours is the kingdom and the power and the glory forever. Amen" (Matthew 6:13b; NIV footnote). This is a threefold doxology of praise. In using it, we give praise that promotes God's kingdom by focusing upon three designations for his kingdom that emphasize different aspects of His reign. As we study this doxology we find that praise promotes God's kingdom, God's power and God's glory.

Praise promotes God's *kingdom*. We are to pray, "Yours is the kingdom." Now we've learned that the term *kingdom* as it is used in the New Testament refers to "sovereignty, royal power, and dominion."(2) When the term is used of God's reign, it refers to "the sphere in which, at any given time, His rule is acknowledged."(3) When we pray, "Yours is the kingdom," we acknowledge God's rule. Therefore, God's kingdom comes to us. When we proclaim in our witnessing, "The kingdom of God is near you" (Luke 10:9), we acknowledge God's rule among those who hear us. Therefore, God's kingdom comes to them to either accept or reject.

We must grasp an important principle here. The *proclamation* of God's kingdom brings the *presence* of God's kingdom. That puts a lot of power in our words. Will we praise God by ascribing to Him "the kingdom" and watch His kingdom materialize? Will we complain about our circumstances and thereby glorify Satan with the result that his kingdom enlarges? We need to keep something in perspective here. Satan may be the god of this world and exercise his kingdom rule in the lives of those who belong to this world. (2 Corinthians 4:4; Luke 16:8.) But we do not belong to this world (John 17:14-16). We are " . . . a people belonging to God, that [we] may declare the praise of him who called [us] out of darkness into his wonderful light" (1 Peter 2:9). We must be a praising people and not a complaining people. Through our praises, we promote God's kingdom.

When we ascribe to God "the kingdom," we come to share in His kingdom. The Bible tells us that we who are born again are incorporated into Christ with the result that we come to "reign in life through the one man, Jesus Christ" (Romans 5:17). Paul states that through our union with Christ, " . . . we are more than conquerors through Him who loved us" (Romans 8:37). Those who praise the King who sits upon the throne will ride upon the high places with Him as they share His kingdom authority. As praise promotes God's kingdom, it brings us to share in God's kingdom authority with the result that we live victorious Christian lives.

We find also that praise promotes God's *power*. We are to pray, "Yours . . . is the power." Now the term for power here is often used to speak of *inherent* ability.(4) Thus God's power may be thought of as of the very essence of God Himself. That is, God's power cannot be separated from God Himself. On at least one occasion, Jesus replaced the designation "God" with the word "power."(5) Consider this passage: "Hereafter shall ye see the Son of man sitting on the right hand of power, and coming in the clouds of heaven" (Matthew 26:64, KJV). The right hand of God is spoken of as "the right hand of power." Now, the translators of the New International Version understood that Jesus was employing a device called *metonymy* in which one designation is replaced with another that is associated with it. Quite possibly to avoid the conclusion that God is a power and not a person, these translators took liberty to render the phrase to read "the right hand of the Mighty *One*" (author's italics). The important point to grasp is that God is a person with inherent power. Therefore, His power is also personal. When we praise God, we promote God's kingdom by promoting His power.

When we praise God by promoting His power, God's power comes to us. And through the exercise of His power we promote God's kingdom in the earth. Note the connection between divine empowerment and the promotion of God's kingdom in this promise of Jesus to His disciples: "But you will receive power when the Holy Spirit comes on you; and you will be my witnesses in Jerusalem, and in all Judea and Samaria, and to the ends of the earth" (Acts 1:8). How was the empowerment of the Holy Spirit to make the disciples Jesus' witnesses? It was to be through the promotion of God's kingdom and the defeat of Satan's kingdom. As Jesus said to His disciples elsewhere, "I have given you authority to trample on snakes and scorpions and to overcome all the power of the enemy; nothing will harm you" (Luke 10:19). The context of this passage shows us that this power against Satan's kingdom was to be used in the disciples' public ministry of promoting God's kingdom. For the promotion of God's power against that of the enemy is kingdom promotion.

As John Wimber reminds us, the promotion of God's kingdom takes places through *power encounters*. This designation "power encounters" was coined by missionary

Alan Tippett and simply means "the clashing of the kingdom of God with the kingdom of Satan".(6) The biblical justification for the concept comes from Luke's gospel where Jesus said, "But if I drive out demons by the finger of God, then the kingdom of God has come to you" (11:20).

I heard John Wimber once relate an example of a power encounter that graphically depicts the superiority of God's power over that of the enemy. He and a team from his church were ministering in England. One evening, they were dining when a glass broke in the hand of a young woman on their team as she was drinking from it. The glass cut her top lip so deeply that blood was pouring. She grabbed a napkin and quickly applied it to her lip. Another team member realized that this whole matter was a work of the devil attempting to cripple their ministry in England. This person blurted at the demon that had caused the injury, "Stop it!" Immediately the bleeding stopped. The napkin was removed to expose a major miracle. Not even a scar remained! The lip was healed.

Consider a similar power encounter.(7) Peter Wagner tells of a missionary who was preaching in an Indonesian village with some success. On one occasion as he was ministering, a well-known witch doctor in the area appeared and challenged the proceedings. In his determination to stop the spread of the gospel, he pointed to a calendar hanging on a nearby wall and said, "Watch the power of my gods, then show me what your God can do!" Instantly the calendar was torn apart by an unseen force. This was, at first, a shock to the missionary who had never witnessed this kind of demonstration of demonic power before. Nonetheless, the missionary had faith in the power of God.

He opened his heart to the Lord and received specific instruction about how to respond. He said to the witch doctor, "The evil spirits always tear things apart and destroy them. But the good God came to correct them and help us." He pointed to the torn calendar. Instantly it was mended without any sign of a tear.

Christians often unintentionally magnify the power of the devil instead of the power of God. When a train of unfavorable circumstances comes their way, you might hear them say, "The devil's really after us today!" This kind of confession plays into the devil's hands. It inadvertently enlarges his power. The antidote to this negative habit pattern is to face unfavorable circumstances with the praises of God on our lips. We must praise God for His power in order to see his power manifest. This is why our prayers should give praise to God by focusing upon His power: "Yours . . . is the power".

As praise promotes God's kingdom and His power, it also promotes His *glory*. We are to pray, "Yours . . . is the glory." Now the glory of God refers to "the manifested perfection of His character".(8) Because God is the epitome of perfection in His character and in His ways, it is fitting that we give Him the glory that is His due.

As with the kingdom and the power of God, the glory of God comes to those who ascribe glory to God in praise. This is illustrated from Scripture in a picturesque manner. (See Exodus 16:10; 25:22; 34:29.) Moses and the people of Israel beheld God's glory regularly. It appeared as a splendor or brightness that emanated from the cloud of God's presence that hovered over the congregation of Israel and over the Holy of Holies. Moses particularly spent long periods of time in the glorious presence of God communing with the Lord as friends would talk face to face. Moses' face became so radiant with the glory of God that he had to cover his face with a veil upon leaving God's presence and returning to the camp of Israel in order to keep from unduly frightening the Israelites.

This participation in the glory of God is not simply an Old Testament phenomenon. It is a phenomenon that is meant to be the experience of all believers. As we ascribe glory to God, we come to share in the glory of God. The Apostle Paul wrote to the Corinthians, "And we, who . . . reflect the Lord's glory, are being transformed into his likeness with ever increasing glory" (2 Corinthians 3:18). The NIV footnote substitutes the word "contemplate" for the word "reflect." The meaning, then, would be this: as we contemplate God's glory, we are clothed with His glory. The effect would be that we reflect God's glory to others and so promote God's kingdom.

When we ascribe glory to God, we are literally being clothed with the glory of God. God taught me this in an unforgetable way when I was in my mid teens. After being baptized in the Holy Spirit, I noticed something peculiar. When I got home from church on Sunday afternoons, I generally went straight to the bathroom, took off my jacket and tie and washed up for lunch. Every week, I noticed that my face had a tangible shine. After noticing this a couple of times, I started rubbing the skin on my face to see if maybe it was excess oil causing the glow. My skin was not oily.

One day, I walked with Bible in hand down to the riverside where I did my Bible reading and prayer. As I strolled, I asked, "Lord, why does my face shine like it does when I come home from church on Sundays?" I really didn't expect an answer.

When I sat down, I turned to the last passage I had read in Acts. (I was reading through the New Testament at the time.) Instead, I decided that I didn't want to read in Acts that day. As I flipped through my Bible, my eyes were drawn to this passage:

> After six days Jesus taketh Peter, James, and John his brother, and bringeth them up into an high mountain apart, And was transfigured before them: *and his face did shine* as the sun, and his raiment was white as the light.—Matthew 17:1,2 (KJV, author's italics).

Suddenly, I had the answer to my prayer! I was experiencing a spiritual transformation that resulted in God's glory, in some limited degree, being tangibly visible in the glow on my face. And why was this glow just visible on Sunday afternoons? Because on Sunday mornings I gathered with God's people to praise Him in lively worship. In praising God, we are tangibly clothed in His glory.

Everett Fullam illustrates this phenomena with an interesting analogy.(9) The moon is not a luminous body. It has no light of its own. But it is clothed with the glory of the sun and reflects that glory to the earth. Likewise, fallen humanity has no glory of its own. Through redemption, we are clothed with God's glory. We are meant to reflect God's glory to the world. Jesus said, "You are the light of the world . . . let your light shine before men, that they may see your good deeds and praise your Father in heaven" (Matthew 5:14,16).

I recently observed a full moon that had a pronounced aura surrounding it. The next evening, the meteorologist on the early evening news pointed out that the full moon the previous night was surrounded by a "halo" that indicated fair weather ahead. This suggested an interesting thought to me that is congruent with Scripture. When our lives reflect the radiance of God's glory, the effect is a clearing of the spiritual atmosphere around us. The glory of God drives out the darkness of Satan's domain. Thus it promotes God's kingdom in the earth.

As we praise God, we are to subscribe to Him glory: "Yours is the glory." As we do, we are clothed in God's glory. The glory of God so transforms our character and our ways that the good deeds of our lives witness to the goodness of our God. This is one way in which God's kingdom comes to the earth. What begins with the praise of God ends in the promotion of His kingdom.

Summing It Up

Praise must be an integral part of our prayer lives. It gives our prayers their proper focus and makes them effective in bringing God's kingdom purposes to bear in our lives and in our world. It is appropriate, then, that our Lord's inspired outline of prayer should end with the three-fold doxology of praise, "For yours is the kingdom and the power and the glory forever. Amen." In our study of praise in the Lord's Prayer and in the closing doxology in particular, we have seen that praise is the key to prayer and to the promotion of God's kingdom.

Praise is the key to prayer. The Lord's Prayer depicts praise as enveloping, enabling and empowering prayer. First, praise envelops prayer in that it both opens and closes prayer. The result is that prayers are focused upon God and His kingdom and are, therefore, prayed in faith rather than according to the emotions of the moment. Second, praise enables prayer in that it brings one into conscious communion with God. When we are conscious of God's presence as we pray, we are assured that He hears and answers our prayers. Thus our prayers are characterized by faith and not fear. Third, praise empowers prayer. When we praise God by ascribing to Him the kingdom, the power and the glory, we loose His kingdom power to grant the petitions that we have offered in prayer. As praise envelops, enables and empowers prayer, it makes for effective prayer that promotes God's kingdom.

Just as praise is the key to prayer, it is also the key to the promotion of God's kingdom. As we ascribe to God "the kingdom," we submit to His reign. The result is that our lives promote His reign. As we ascribe to God "the power," we are empowered for ministry. The result is that our ministries demonstrate the superiority of God's power over that of the enemy. As we ascribe to God "the glory," we are clothed in God's glory. The result is that the good deeds of our lives bring glory to God and so promote His kingdom.

It is fitting that the final note of our study of the Lord's Prayer should emphasize the purpose and the importance of praise. I trust that our reflections together in this chapter will motivate each of us to give the praise of God its proper place in our prayers. As we do, we will find that our prayers effectively promote God's kingdom in the earth.

Notes

1. Merlin R. Carothers, *Power In Praise,* (Escondido, California: Merlin R. Carothers, 1972), pp. 3,4.

2. W. E. Vine, "An Expository Dictionary of New Testament Words," in *Vine's Expository Dictionary of Biblical Words,* Edited by W. E. Vine, Merrill F. Unger and William White, Jr. (Nashville: Thomas Nelson Publishers, 1985), p. 344.

3. Ibid.

4. W. E. Vine, p. 2.

5. Ibid., p. 478.

6. John Wimber and Kevin Springer, *Power Evangelism* (New York: Harper Collins Publishers, 1986), p. 16.

7. From *The Third Wave of the Holy Spirit,* Copyright © 1988 by C. Peter Wagner. Published by Servant Publications, Box 8617, Ann Arbor, Michigan 48107. Used by Permission, pp. 42,43.

8. W. E. Vine, p. 267.

9. Everett L. Fullam with Bob Slosser, *Living The Lord's Prayer* (Old Tappan, New Jersey: Fleming H. Revell Company, 1980), p. 131.

Conclusion

In our study of the Lord's Prayer, we have endeavored to understand the meaning of the prayer as a whole, and of each petition in particular in the context of Scripture and of life. While our study has been by no means comprehensive, I trust that the insights we have presented have contributed toward motivating and enabling you to pray the prayer with greater understanding and spiritual sensitivity. I encourage you to take what you have gleaned from this study and apply it to your prayer life on a consistent, daily basis. As you do, I believe that your prayer life will be enriched with the result that you will experience in greater measure victorious Christian living. You will discover the truth contained in these wise words of a devoted, faithful missionary: "Much prayer, much power; little prayer, little power; no prayer, no power!"

Perhaps you have read this book with benefit but still find it difficult to develop a disciplined and consistent prayer life. It may be that your prayers have too often been ineffectual with the result that you have become frustrated to the point of minimizing your time spent in prayer. Such frustration may even have reduced you to a state of prayerlessness. Such lack of motivation and frustration in prayer will be alleviated as you develop the discipline of making the Lord's Prayer the basis of your prayer life. When you make this inspired prayer of Scripture the model and outline for your praying, you will be praying according to God's will and in line with His kingdom priorities. Such prayer will always be effectual.

If the humble and sincere cry of our hearts is that of the original disciples of Jesus—"Lord, teach us to pray . . ." (Luke 11:1), then Jesus' answer to our hearts' cry was given when He gave us in the Lord's Prayer his inspired outline of prayer. As we follow the outline, we will learn to pray. This outline of prayer instructs us in four ways.

First, the Lord's Prayer gives *structure* to our praying. We worship God through reverence, adoration and the acknowledgment of His covenant names that communicate the nature of His relationship with us and the blessings He bestows upon us. Then we pray for the coming of His kingdom in order that His will be accomplished in our lives and through our lives in the world. Then we petition Him for the meeting of our needs for provision, pardon and protection. Finally, we close our prayers with praise that promotes God's kingdom by ascribing to our Sovereign Lord the kingdom, the power, and the glory. This four-part structure for prayer need not straightjacket our prayer lives, though it will effectively impose God's priorities upon our prayers. We will not meander in aimless praying that inevitably produces the frustration of ineffectual prayer.

Second, the Lord's Prayer gives *content* to our prayers. Jesus' master outline of prayer not only tells us *how* to pray, but also *what* to pray. Each petition of the Lord's Prayer suggests the content for that part of the prayer while leaving it to us to follow the direction of the Holy Spirit in the development of the prayer. For instance, the Lord's Prayer requires that we hallow God's name. But it leaves it to us to decide whether to hallow His name as our Father, our Savior, our Lord or in accordance with any of the covenant names given in the Old Testament and fulfilled in the New Testament in the incarnate God, Jesus Christ. Likewise, the Lord's Prayer requires that we pray for the coming of God's kingdom to earth. But, we may be led of God's Spirit to pray this petition one day from the perspective of evangelizing the lost and to pray it another day from the vantage point of social ministry to the poor and needy. While allowing us freedom to follow the direction of the Holy Spirit in articulating our prayers, our Lord's prayer outline provides guidelines that give content to our prayers.

Third, the Lord's Prayer gives *comprehensiveness* to our prayers. We said in our introduction that this inspired outline of prayer addresses all of God and lays before Him all of life as it draws upon the grace of God the Father to provide, God the Son to forgive and God the Holy Spirit to protect. Furthermore, the prayer elicits from us responsiveness in worship, evangelism, social ministry, mutual forgiveness, dependence upon God's care and praise. In such a short outline of prayer, Jesus has shown us how to assure that our prayers are truly comprehensive.

Finally, the Lord's Prayer gives *practicality* to our prayers. This is a prayer that invites God to equip us for action. Its central theme is the kingdom of God. And how does the kingdom of God go forth? Through our anointed ministries fulfilling the evangelistic mandate and the social mandate. As we hallow God's name and pray for the coming of His kingdom, we must bear His name and His kingdom to others in a life of active ministry so that the lost will be saved and the needy adequately supplied.

I trust that you have gained a sense of appreciation for the value of the Lord's Prayer while reading *After This Manner, Pray*. Let me encourage you to utilize the Lord's Prayer as a prayer outline in two ways. First, pray it verbatim and reflectively from time to time, allowing the Holy Spirit to speak to you through each petition of the prayer. Second, make it the basis for your prayer life by following the direction of the Holy Spirit in elaborating upon its various petitions. Both of these approaches may be combined with profit in the dialogue of prayer.

Our prayer track is before us. Jesus has given it to us in the Lord's Prayer. Let us discipline ourselves in daily prayer to run it for all it is worth. As we do, our prayer lives will be both effectual and delightful as we discover in prayer the key to victorious Christian living. Furthermore, our prayers will become a mighty tool by which God brings about the establishment of His kingdom in the earth for our good and for His glory.

BIBLIOGRAPHY

Adams, Jay E. *Sibling Rivalry in the Household of God.* Denver, Colorado: Accent Books, 1988.

Allee, John Gage, ed. *Webster's Encyclopedia of Dictionaries.* U.S.A.: Ottenheimer Publishers, Inc., 1958.

Barclay, William *The Gospel of Matthew,* Revised edition, The Daily Bible Study Series, Vol. 2. Philadelphia: The Westminster Press; Edinburgh: The Saint Andrew Press, 1975.

Bennett, Rita. *Inner Wholeness Through The Lord's Prayer.* Tarrytown, New York: Fleming H. Revell Company, 1991.

Bjorge, James R. *Living In The Forgiveness Of God.* Minneapolis: Augsburg, Fortress, 1990.

Carothers, Merlin R. *Power In Praise.* Escondido, California: Merlin R. Carothers, 1972.

Cho, Paul Yonggi. *The Fourth Dimension.* Plainfield, New Jersey: Logos International, 1979.

Cho, Paul Yonggi. *Praying With Jesus.* Altamonte Springs, Florida: Creation House, 1987.

Duffield, Guy P., and N. M. Van Cleave. *Foundations of Pentecostal Theology*. Los Angeles: Life Bible College, 1983.

France, R. T. *Matthew*. Leicester and Grand Rapids: InterVarsity Press and William B. Eerdmans Publishing Company, 1985.

Fullam, Everett, and Bob Slosser. *Living the Lord's Prayer*. Old Tappan, New Jersey: Fleming H. Revell Company, 1980.

Hagin, Kenneth E. *The Believer's Authority*. 2nd ed. Tulsa: Faith Library Publications, 1984.

Kelly, Douglas F., and Caroline S. Kelly. *If God Already Knows, Why Pray?* Brentwood, Tennessee: Woglumuth & Hyatt, Publishers, Inc., 1989.

Ladd, George Eldon. *A Theology of the New Testament*. Grand Rapids, Michigan: William B. Eerdman's Publishing Company, 1974.

Lawson, Steven. "Defeating Territorial Spirits." *Charisma*, April 1990, pp. 47-55.

Lea, Larry. *Could You Not Tarry One Hour?* Lake Mary, Florida: Creation House, 1987.

L'Engle, Madeleine. *The Irrational Season*. New York: Harper Collins Publishers, 1977.

McPherson, Anna Talbott. *They Dared To Be Different*. Chicago: Moody Press, 1967.

Muller, George. *The Autobiography of George Muller*. Springdale, Pennsylvania: Whitaker House, 1984.

Murray, Andrew. *The Prayer Life*. Springdale, Pennsylvania: Whitaker House, 1981.

Price, Frederick K. C. *Is Healing For All?*. Tulsa: Harrison House, 1976.

Robertson, Pat., and Bob Slosser. *The Secret Kingdom*. Nashville: Thomas Nelson Publishers, 1982.

Robertson, Pat, and William Proctor. *Beyond Reason: How Miracles Can Change Your Life*. New York: Bantam Books,1984.

Signs And Wonders Today. Compiled by the Editors of Christian Life Magazine in cooperation with C. Peter Wagner, Professor of Church Growth, Fuller Theological Seminary. Wheaton, Illinois: Christian Life Missions, 1983.

Stanley, Charles. *Temptation*. Nashville: Thomas Nelson Publishers, 1988.

Vine, W. E. "An Expository Dictionary of New Testament Words." *Vine's Expository Dictionary of Biblical Words.* W. E. Vine, Merrill F. Unger and William White. Nashville: Thomas Nelson Publishers, 1985.

Wagner, C. Peter. *How To Have A Healing Ministry Without Making Your Church Sick.* Ventura, California: Regal Books, 1988.

Wagner, C. Peter. *The Third Wave of the Holy Spirit.* Ann Arbor, Michigan: Servant Publications, 1988.

Wesley, John. *The Nature of the Kingdom.* Ed. Clare George Weakley, Jr. Minneapolis: Bethany House Publishers, 1979.

Whitehead, John W. *The Stealing of America.* Westchester, Pennsylvania: Crossway Books, 1983.

Whyte, H. A. Maxwell. *Demons and Deliverance.* Springdale, Pennsylvania: Whitaker House, 1989.

Wiersbe, Warren W. *The Bible Exposition Commentary.* Vol. 1. Wheaton: Victor Books, 1989.

Wigglesworth, Smith. *Ever Increasing Faith.* Rev. ed. Springfield: Gospel Publishing House, 1971.

Wimber, John. *Kingdom Come.* Ann Arbor, Michigan: Servant Publications, 1988.

Wimber, John, and Kevin Springer. *Power Evangelism.* New York: Harper Collins Publishers, 1986.

Young, Robert. "Index-Lexicon To The New Testament." *Young's Analytical Concordance to The Bible.* 22nd American ed. Grand Rapids, Michigan: William B. Eerdmans Publishing Company, 1970.

The author may be reached at the following address:

J. Mark Copeland
P.O. Box 453
Suffolk, VA 23439